Ba

MW00945729

SURVIVING PROVENCE

**Romance, Reality
and Wild Boars**

illustrations by Susanne Strassmann

ISBN: 9781976858697

Author's Notes

Surviving Provence is a humorous account of the people (and animals) who share our daily life in the South of France. It is a far cry from an ode to lavender and sunflowers.

Although my husband and I were both born in the United States, we have spent the greater part of our lives in Europe, mostly in The Netherlands. Leaving our working years and Amsterdam behind us, we settled into our huge white elephant of a house in Provence. The house had been ours for 20 years but only as a destination for summer vacations. As a friend told us, "You live in a fool's paradise until you come here to reside permanently." And was he right! Living here full time is a combination of love, frustration and amazement.

When the chicken man at our local market scolded me for not reserving one of his roasted delicacies in advance, and the flower vendor told me if I cut flowers from my garden the stars would cry, I knew our life had changed. Complaining that our olive trees were not producing very much, our Portuguese/French tree cutter suggested I talk to them. He was serious and I did. The next year we had 400 kilos of olives.

Rabbits and wild boars destroy our well-manicured grass. The post office lady in her yellow car gives cookies to our three dogs when she delivers our mail. A small dog drinks beer at a local café with his master. The pharmacist gives me a recommendation for my wrinkles, in a voice loud enough for all his clients to profit from. I learn some quaint French expressions from the plumber, not however, to be used in polite society. Our tennis pro collects shirts, like others do stamps. A longhaired hippie cries because he is cutting down a dead tree. There are encounters with temperamental painters, carpenters, masons, hunters, firemen and spiritual beekeepers.

Relations with their neighbors brings out the combative instinct in the French. There are clashes about water and property lines, but also absurd issues such as a hairdresser's dispute over a whistling parrot, the unjust case of stolen figs and a smoking pizza oven among others.

Of course food and wine play an important role in the book. The French have very precise eating and drinking habits, quite different from our Anglo-Saxon ways. There are no restaurant recommendations, only wonderful Provençal recipes from a friend, some with a delightful literary twist. There are also descriptions of disastrous dinner parties, mine, as well as some to which we have been invited.

The house is the star of the book. It is a perfect example of Andy Warhol's fifteen minutes of fame, becoming much better known than its owners. It has been a setting for TV soup commercials. Oversized women's clothes for a Swiss mail order catalogue were photographed in the garden, supervised by the oversize Swiss client. Fashion photography of very chic men's underwear brought us a sexy Los Angeles male model, who posed in very minimal shorts, outside in November, smiling and shivering the whole time. The newest model of Peugeot was unveiled on our terrace. Several TV series, almost always involving a murder or kidnapping, brought film crews for weeks.

This is just a taste of what awaits you in Surviving Provence. I hope, dear reader, you will enjoy this book as much as I did writing it. It is meant to make you smile.

Barbara Farber

To Jules, who throughout our long life together, has always encouraged me to do the things I thought I could not.

And to Mark, Jay and Alicia whose love and support enlighten all my days.

With thanks to:

Mike Lotzof. His technical expertise, creativity, sense of humor and persistence turned a manuscript into a book.

Susanne Strassmann. Her wonderful illustrations have caught the spirit of the book. They have added a delightful note.

And special thanks to all the characters in the book, real and unreal.

When the Good Lord begins to doubt the world, he remembers that he created Provence.

Frederic Mistral

CONTENTS

IN THE BEGINNING

With the heart and the temperament of a Latin, I have spent most of my life in a northern country. As American expatriates, my husband and I lived for some 35 years in Amsterdam – a city not famous for its climate, although widely admired for a host of other attributes – 17th century houses lining picturesque canals, music, art, modernity and, of course, great weed. Our escape from the cultural, Calvinistic, combined with an over the top freedom, of The Netherlands was a house in Provence, everyone's dream. Admittedly, twenty-five years ago when we bought the huge white elephant in which we now reside, Provence was not quite as "in" as it is now.

But life in our southern "retreat" was limited to summer vacation, an occasional week at Christmas or Easter, not total Provençal immersion. A friend once told us, "Until you live here full time, you are in a fool's paradise." Those words, unfortunately so true, have come back time and again to haunt me. Things work a little differently in Provence than in Amsterdam, pleasures as well as tribulations.

Finally, the day arrived, coinciding with a certain age, when we decided to change our lives. The word retirement was a four-letter word, figuratively, and never uttered. We were just going to live another life in the sunny South. My husband, when asked his profession had always replied, "I'm a writer." Although he did publish a few books, in fact, he ran an extremely successful and profitable public relations office. Now, he could finally be what he always claimed he was.

On a typical Dutch rainy day at the end of June, we closed the door to our Amsterdam house, loaded the car with suitcases and left for Provence, as we had done every year for the past 10 years. But this time was different. It was to be forever. Our golden years, our *troisieme age* (third age) as the French so delicately put it, the senior way of life – all phrases I detest with fervor – were going to be spent in Provence.

A decade has gone by.

CHAPTER 1

THE HOUSE

Love at first sight is a dangerous concept. It makes one oblivious to the blatant and hidden faults of the object of one's desire. Bad enough when choosing a partner, although there are exceptions to every rule. At 15, I zoomed in on J and we have been married for a zillion years but when it comes to houses, passionate, blind love can lead to unimagined catastrophes. That's why sane buyers rationally look for the defects, hire architects and engineers to check over the prospective abode, comparison shop houses in the same price category, bring in knowledgeable friends and brothers-in-law to confirm their decision. No one in their right mind just walks onto a property and says, "We'll take it." Except us.

We had a lovely house north of Aix-en-Provence with an exceptionally green garden, most unusual in dry Provence. Everything grew, the grass verdant, vegetables in abundance. Water, water everywhere, bubbling out of a lion's mouth, a nymph's urn, a spitting god into 18th century fountains and also seeping through all our floors, up the walls and sometimes descending from the ceiling. After 10 years of scrubbing the moss off the tiles in the living room, I looked up one Easter morning at J from my usual kneeling position – no, not in church, on the floor – and said, "That's it! Sell it!" Two weeks later it was sold, to our regret and amazement, to a couple who fell in love with it at first sight. Actually, so had we.

Being so used to having a second home in sunny Provence to compensate for our normal life in rainy, cold Amsterdam, we asked the agent who had so successfully sold our waterlogged, beloved house to find us another one but smaller a. s. a. p. A few weeks later, he phoned assuring us he had the absolutely perfect property for us. "You must come immediately. Such a house will be snapped up right away, but I will do my best to keep it for you." We were on the next plane to Marseille.

The marvel was a smaller version of our old house. Much smaller, a Lilliputian remake. Two people couldn't pass in the upstairs hall and J needed to duck through all the doorways.

He was also quite furious. "Is there possibly something else you can show us?"

"You don't like it?" asked our agent. "It is a very dry house."

He made it clear he had nothing further, which could conceivably be suitable for such difficult people, and brought us back to the hotel. With a non-refundable return ticket to Amsterdam and nowhere to go, no one to see, we decided to spend Saturday morning window-shopping the realtors on the Cours

Mirabeau in Aix. The first agency we passed had a photo of an absolute dream house in the window. We went in and were greeted by a smiling, portly, very Provençal gentleman, *Monsieur* Thierry. Of course, he would take us that very afternoon to view the house, although he warned he had not yet visited it himself. In case the house should be a disappointment, he would show us other things he thought we might like.

J wanted to give him a very specific description of what we were looking for, but I whispered in his ear to just go with the flow. I never know what I really want until I see it. The dream house turned out to be rather attractive, spoiled by a sort of thermal reactor in the backyard spewing clouds of what, I can only hope, was not some sort of nuclear waste *Monsieur* Thierry assured us it was only making energy from coal and apologized profusely for having brought us to a property, "admittedly not to everyone's taste" Certainly, not ours!

We spent the next few hours visiting various houses ranging from undistinguished to downright awful. One was situated so near the local railway tracks J could have applied for a job as station-master. Another situated high on a hill approachable by a narrow, curved unpaved road offered a panoramic vista of the gas station below.

By this time it had started to rain, *Monsieur* Thierry was beginning to look very sad and J was extremely bored. "I have one more *grande propriété* (large property) to show you, although it really is not what you are looking for. It is too big, too run down, too expensive and the owner is totally impossible to deal with." J gave me that "great!" look but I was desperate and determined to find something.

We drove up to an enormous faded ochre house, paint peeling in all directions, shutters hanging askew, a huge dirt terrace sprouting weeds of incredible varieties but with a view of the majesty of the Montagne Sainte Victoire on one side, the Mount Olympe and Aurelian on the other, and eight regal plane trees towering above all those weeds. A fountain, nestled on the edge of the terrace, spewed water through the mouth of a strange stone creature into a large pool filled with goldfish. That was it! J and I looked at each other. Love at first sight!

This vast house, three stories high, with ten bedrooms, had but one occupant, *Madame* Boulet. Although a bit stout and frumpily dressed, one could very easily imagine how beautiful she must have been as a young woman. Still an imposing lady of a certain age – younger at the time then we are now – she greeted us politely, scanned us closely with amazing green eyes and took an immediate affinity to J. "You are American?" she asked. "And Jewish?" How she divined this still remains a mystery. "Good, I like that. I, too, have Jewish blood, although, of course, I am Catholic. Perhaps this house was meant for you." Perhaps? It had been on the market for five years.

The inside of the house was amazing, incredibly proportioned, with high ceilings even in the third floor bedrooms, large paned windows and doors opening from the grand living room onto a raised terrace overlooking the Sainte Victoire. The walls were painted in the colors of Provence, ochre, terra cotta, grey-green. That is to say where there was still some paint left. She proudly showed us the lines on the wall in the living room which had been marked off to measure her height starting when she was 3 years old. She was now well over 60.

A monumental staircase with an intricate wrought iron banister wound its elegant way up through the three floors. From the immense front hall, you could look up for about 20 meters. Talk about cathedral ceilings. Also climbing up and right through the roof was a metal pipe connected to a gas burning potbellied stove in the middle of the hall, next to *Madame*'s bed. Although the house did have a central heating system, as evidenced by the many old fashioned, but very decorative radiators and the visible pipes connected to them, *Madame* Boulet was extremely frugal, by necessity, and never turned on the heat. In fact, except for the hall where she slept, the dining room, which was her office and had a wood burning fireplace, and a miserable kitchen, she never used any other part of the house. But every inch of the place was crammed with furniture, books, lamps, bibelots and masses of just plain junk. *Monsieur* Thierry discreetly whispered that most of the good stuff had been sold to various antique dealers.

The two upstairs floors with their long halls had the feeling of a provincial hotel long past its prime. Each bedroom was the size of an expensive modern apartment's living room. Threadbare silk wall coverings hung in shreds, but the ceilings were unscarred by water damage. After our last house experience, this was a big plus point. Each bedroom had its own bathroom attached, with windows and wonderful views, but not exactly in a condition to take a hot bath in.

Besides the huge house comprising 250 square meters per floor, there was a greenhouse for overwintering plants, which probably had not seen a plant in 50 years considering the amount of debris in it, an enormous cave once used to store and make wine, some very dilapidated rooms over it to house the grape pickers during the *vendange*, (harvest) and an Art Deco *colombier* (dovecote), originally for white doves, but which had been turned into more practical use with wire-enclosed chicken and rabbit runs. There were eight animal apartments, four on each side of a lofty tower residence, decorated with tiles, for doves (or perhaps carrier pigeons). It was, we supposed, in its time, a very elegant way of keeping the food supply but despite its fancy name, by which *Madame* Boulet insisted on calling it, it was pretty much of a ruin. We referred to it as the pigeon house and the name has stuck to it for the last 25 years, even after its renovation. The rest of the almost four hectares could only be described as overgrown, to put it mildly. A Provençal jungle.

The tour of the house took well over two hours. *Madame* Boulet, refusing to be interrupted by any practical questions, treated us to a monologue of the house's history, importance, beauty and emphasized that she would not sell it to just anyone. *Monsieur* Thierry followed meekly. J and I tried to conceal our enthusiasm – not good for negotiating. Finally, we were back in the hall, totally overwhelmed and exhausted. *Madame* Boulet fixed us with her sharp eyes and said: "I will sell you my house. You are worthy of it. No one but my family has ever lived in it." With that, she shook my hand, gave J a kiss on both cheeks and showed us the door.

"It's too big," said J once we were back in the car.

"We'll close off the third floor," I replied.

"There's too much work to be done," noted J.

"I know an excellent mason," answered *Monsieur* Thierry.

"Well, it's too damn expensive, that's for sure," J again.

Monsieur Thierry: "I will negotiate a good price for you. She needs to sell but it is true she is very proud and has refused other buyers."

We drove back to Aix in a state of exaltation and despair. What were we letting ourselves in for? How would we ever redo such a huge monster, both inside and outside? Was the roof sound? The electricity? The plumbing? What mystic force was drawing us into this foolhardy adventure, a sure recipe for disaster.

"This has been a very long day for you," sympathized *Monsieur* Thierry. "For me it is not unusual. It is my *metier* (profession). May I invite you to come to dinner at my home tonight. I know my wife is making a *bouillabaisse*. (renowned Provençal fish soup). She is a true Marseillaise and her *bouillabaisse* is better than any you will ever eat at the port. Also, I will tell you the history of your new house and of *Madame* Boulet. It is very special."

We accepted with delight. "Our new house?" We hadn't even as yet discussed the price. But we knew it was a *fait accompli* (done deal). I must also add that *Monsieur* Thierry was anything but a pushy real estate agent trying to unload a white elephant. I am extremely pragmatic and not at all prone to mysticism, but I knew there were strong forces out there and I don't mean commercial ones. I will tell you more about the strange coincidences regarding the house later on in the chapter.

Monsieur Thierry lived in a normal-sized Provençal house with his charming wife who insisted we drop the *Madame* and call her Elizabeth.

"I know in America, everyone uses first names very quickly. In Provence, we are not so formal as the rest of France," she laughed.

In contrast to her very round husband, she was tall, slim and unexpectedly fashionable as French women can be. I felt like a frumpy, rumpled second cousin after the whole day of house hunting. Over a very welcome glass of pastis, *Monsieur* Thierry explained he had followed his father into the agency and expected his son would do the same, which in fact he did several years later.

Bouillabaisse, the visiting card of Marseille cuisine, made of the cheapest rock fish, simmered with onions, garlic, spices and heads and tails of all sorts of other sea animals, is a delicacy. It is accompanied by rouille, a sort of garlic mayonnaise made with saffron, pimento, and more garlic than should be legally allowed, which is spread on crispy croutons and thrown in the strained broth. You can't breathe on anyone for days after. An immediate siesta usually follows the feast. But not this evening. After the remains of the soup had been cleared away, (I had to poke J to stop him from licking his plate) and we were into a sumptuous cheese platter, *Monsieur* Thierry began the saga of the house.

It had been built as a country retreat by a famous and wealthy lawyer, *Monsieur* Emile Séguret, the grandfather of *Madame* Boulet, at the end of the 19th century. He had an impressive residence on the Cours Mirabeau in Aix-en-Provence and his rural abode was more dignified than rustic. As a lawyer and intellectual, he travelled widely and was especially enamored of all things Italian, so I suppose he gave the architect some instructions on how to give his new abode a Florentine touch.

Believe me, it is not, however, in any way a Palladian villa! He also acquired all the land in the surrounding area, approximately 100 hectares, which gave him ownership of half of the encircling mountains. He planted vines, the cultivation of wine being a rich man's diversion in those times. He was very active in Jewish affairs in Aix and married a beautiful girl, a good bit younger than he, Emma Milhaud from a prominent Jewish family. They had two children, one of whom would be the mother of *Madame* Boulet. So, there was the explanation of Jewish blood. In fact, *Madame* Boulet was totally Jewish and was hidden with her mother during the Vichy regime. After the war, she converted to Catholicism.

Monsieur Séguret left the house to his daughter when he died, who in turn passed it on to *Madame* Boulet. She married a double -named aristocrat from a family who had made a fortune producing soap, Savon de Marseille. He was *le fils à papa* which means he lived off the family riches and never worked a day in his life. The marriage was not a happy one. The debonair gentleman of leisure left her with two daughters, and not much else, preferring the cosmopolitan social life in the port city with his young secretary to the quiet existence of a *vigneron* (winemaker). *Madame* Boulet was made of strong stock. Undaunted she took over the cultivation of the 40 hectares of vines with a passion for which she was famous in the whole region.

She was also famous in the village for various idiosyncrasies, one being the relation with the local butcher. Dressed in her *peignor,* (dressing gown) she would drive up in her old Citroen *deux chevaux,* park in front of the shop, blocking traffic, honk her horn and when the obliging butcher came out, she would hand him her list. A few minutes later he would reappear with a very small package. "Add it to my bill," she would command. The local gossip had it that the bill was rarely paid.

"Did you notice the last bedroom, she showed us?" asked *Monsieur* Thierry.

Indeed, we had but since *Madame* Boulet didn't seem to be taking questions, we remained silent and just looked. To our amazement, in contrast to the stuffy, classic decoration in the rest of the house, this room was painted purple, orange and brown. Posters of the Beatles and Jimi Hendrix adorned the walls. A white summer dress was thrown over a bright green chair. The ambience was sixties hippy.

"It was the room of Margot," explained *Monsieur* Thierry," her youngest daughter. She committed suicide in that room. *Madame* Boulet has never gotten over it," he continued. "It is one of the reasons it is so difficult for her to sell the house."

Monsieur brought us to our hotel, gave us a very special bottle of Pastis to take back to Amsterdam, in the days when you could still carry liquids on planes

16

and asked one last question, very discreetly. "What would you like to pay for the house?" J, never one shy in bargaining, named a price far below the asking one. I wanted to sink through the floor.

"Yes," replied our unflappable agent, "that'sfair. You will have the house for that amount. I know *Madame* Boulet very well. I will convince her." With a final handshake and a *dormez bien* (sleep well), he revved up his car and vanished into the night.

"Sleep well!!!" We didn't close an eye. J was furious with himself. "What a fool I am! I should have offered much less. It's his French charm. We are probably overpaying. We could have gotten it cheaper."

After 15 minutes of this raving, I sat straight up in bed, fixed J with a mean eye and told him, "If we get the house for the amount you agreed to, it will be the biggest bargain of your life. Good night!"

It took more than six months of patient negotiating on the part of *Monsieur* Thierry who reported progress faithfully every week or so. The price was the least of the stumbling blocks. More daunting were the conditions *Madame* Boulet was imposing. She wanted to keep the cave in *jouissance* (hers to use) until not only her death but to that of her remaining daughter who must have been 35 at the time. She also wanted the rooms above the cave for the workers during the *vendange* despite the fact that she hadn't produced wine for years. The lilac bushes, which were the only civilized plants on the property, were not to be part of the deal, since she was planning on digging them up and replanting them in the garden of her daughter's new house where she would now live. And we must buy the huge mirror in one of the bedrooms. The lilacs and the mirror, we agreed to. Her indeterminate presence and that of her daughter was something else. We finally acquiesced to her keeping the right to the cave only until her death. Actually, in the end, its only purpose was to house her two Citroen *deux chevaux* – one ancient and one new and unused, but ready in case of the demise of the former. She never drove either one again.

Finally, the day came for the signing of the deed. *Madame* Boulet was at her most elegant, style 1950s, and carrying a Hermes bag now sought after in vintage boutiques. She was accompanied by her more fashionable, Chanel attired, but much less charming, daughter. The ceremony took place in the office of her *notaire*. (In France, the notaire is an extremely important person, dealing with property sales as well as a myriad of other legal matters involving inheritance, wills, etc. No relation to an American notary.) We also had a *notaire* there representing our interests. It took eight hours, not including an hour for lunch, while *Madame* Boulet checked every last word of the contract, disputing, changing and correcting various phrases. Not for nothing was she the granddaughter of a renowned lawyer. She had obviously inherited his nitty-gritty legal mind. Although J and I are both reasonably fluent in French, after a while we had the feeling of being spectators of a very dramatic but incomprehensible French play.

The biggest bone of contention was the name of the property. *Madame* Boulet had long sold off the vineyards and the adjoining farm bearing the name Chateau Ferry La Combe to *Monsieur* Bertrand, a rich Parisian looking for a hobby. And the wine he produced was under this name. She had signed a paper in which she relinquished all rights to the name as well as all variations on it. Nevertheless, she insisted that her house be sold to us with its original name: Le Chateau de la Combe. Her *notaire* produced the original copy of the document and informed her this was absolutely not possible.

"It is the name of the house," she proclaimed, and is written that way in the official records. And that is the way it will be transferred." Fixing both of the very prestigious guardians of French law with a glacial stare, she admonished, "You are too young to know everything. In this you are wrong, and the house will keep its name. Now just get on with it." And if you can believe it, they did.

The footnote to that decision was a court case against us by the owner of the neighboring wine chateau. He was furious that she had not sold him the house, for which he had first right of refusal. The house would have satisfied his illusions of grandeur. Instead, he had the vines and a farmhouse but not the real impressive manor. She managed this by informing him she would only sell the house to him if she had the right to stay in it until not only her death, but that of her daughter as well. In selling to us, this condition was completely waived.

As revenge, he accused us of all sorts of misdemeanors. We were taking orders for wine by telephone and not passing them on to him. We had placed large signs at the beginning of the road pointing to our house as the source of his wine. And on and on. At the time we were still living in Amsterdam, we had an unlisted French telephone number, and the only signs were building permits for construction on our house.

The legal process continued for years and finally reached *le Cours de Cassation* the highest French court. At this point *Madame* Boulet was dead, and *Monsieur* Bertrand was no longer the owner, having sold the chateau years before. French law at its strangest. This caprice ended up costing us thousands of francs to defend a name we couldn't have cared less about and were perfectly willing to change. And change it we finally did, since the supreme court of the land ruled against us.

It is not easy to think of a new name for a house after you have known it. It's hard enough to name a child or a dog. Finally, our very good friend, Count Alain de Montfort, whose noble family had lived in the village for over 500 years suggested we call it Chateau Vallat, *vallat* meaning valley in Provençal. Since indeed we are surrounded by mountains, this seemed logical, and so we changed our letterhead and that was that. Years later, we discovered the name had connotations of which we could never have dreamed.

When *Madame* Boulet died, we were surprised and sad. Always in robust health, we often joked that she would outlive us, and we would never recuperate the cave. Although she had been a not- always- welcome part of our lives during the years we only used the house in the summer, we were attached to her. Extremely curious and most probably sentimental, she kept finding excuses to come around and investigate what changes were being made.

Her advice was free and profuse. Her disapproval of certain things was far from discreet. The hatred for the neighbors to whom she had sold the vineyards was virulent and there was always some court case against them initiated by her for real or imagined transgressions. As an *agriculteur,* (farmer) her insurance paid lawyers" fees. Not that she needed them. Her own legal skills were formidable. J remained her favorite. She always managed to guide him somewhere away from the house ostensibly to show a hidden well on the property, or where she had kept bees as a young women. Sometimes, it was to give him practical advice how to drain off the excess water in the driveway and detailed instructions on dealing with the "unscrupulous" owner of the vineyard next door.

Madame Boulet was buried in the family tomb on what had once been her property but now belonged to the despised owners to whom she had sold the vineyards. In fact, it is forbidden to bury anyone on private property, but this tomb had existed since the death of *Monsieur* Séguret in 1921. He is buried there, along with his wife, Emma, *Madame* Boulet's unfortunate daughter, and strangely enough *Madame* Boulet's ex-husband who died long after they were divorced.

The tomb is hidden in a patch of woods. Actually, it is an obelisk with the names of the dead engraved on the stone. We often visit *Madame* Boulet. Even the dogs know the way to the tomb and are very respectful, never ever peeing anywhere near it. This may sound absurd, but it is true. Our youngest grandchild was very curious to know where the bodies went. I suppose there is a way but I couldn't answer that question. All that's visible is the obelisk.

To our great surprise and a bit of chagrin, we noticed a slight change in the obelisk after *Madame* Boulet had been interred. The Star of David carved into the stone at the time of *Monsieur* Séguret's death had been covered over with a marble plaque. The Star of David had been replaced by a cross. Her daughter, always denying any Jewish blood, had obliterated the traces of it from the family grave.

Shortly after *Madame* Boulet's death, we received a telephone call from what we thought, judging from her somewhat childish voice, was a young girl, asking if she could visit us. "I am writing about the life of Emile Séguret and I would love to see the house he built and lived in." How nice, we thought. Someone young interested in the rather obscure history of our house.

"Of course," replied J. "When would you like to come?"

"Tomorrow," was the unhesitant reply.

In his usual enthusiastic fashion, without so much as a glance in my direction, he set the time and proceeded to give directions to the house.

"Probably a student," said J, ignoring my protests, "and needs to get it done quickly for a term paper."

The next day promptly at 2 o'clock our "student" arrived, breathless from having hiked the five kilometers from the bus stop to our house – in thongs! Despite the childish voice, Suzanne Dupont was anything but young. Pushing 60 in one direction or another, she resembled nothing so much as a left-over flower child from Haight Ashbury. Grey hair streaming over her shoulders, and dressed in a flowing garment with various necklaces of colored beads wound around her neck, she looked at us and the house through huge red framed glasses. Two large tears left her eyes.

"So, this is where he lived. He touched this with his hands" running hers over the stair banister. "This is what he saw when he looked out of the window," regarding with awe our view of the Sainte Victoire. I quickly gave her a glass of iced tea, hoping this would calm the overflowing emotions brought about by our house.

J who is not overly sensitive to extreme feminine emotions immediately began interrogating her. Why was she so interested in Emile Séguret? Was she writing a book? What was her occupation? Author? How had she found us?

Apparently calmed by a cold drink, she told us she was a professor of law at the university, but her hobby was researching and writing about exceptional people who had had an influence in the region of Aix-en-Provence. She had published several very erudite works and, as we later found out, was an extremely well-respected historian. You can't judge by appearances!

Of course, she wanted to see the tomb. With the three dogs accompanying us, we set off. Looking at me, she said "You know, he is very happy you have this house. He is walking with us. I can feel it. You are the first people to live in his house who are not his descendants. But you are Jewish, so you belong to his extended family. He was very worried when his granddaughter was planning to sell the house, but now he is tranquil. He is smiling down at us." My spiritual imagination is very limited, and this conversation was beginning to feel spooky. I am not a great believer in after-life. But then again, maybe Suzanne had links to heaven I did not.

After all this other worldly talk, she suddenly stopped, eyes fixed on mine. "Why did you change the name of your house to Chateau Vallat. I told her about the court case. "But why did you choose that name?" "It was suggested by a good friend," I explained.

"Did you ever hear of Xavier Vallat?"

"No," I replied.

"Well," continued Suzanne, "he was *Commissaire Général aux questions juive* (High Commissioner for the Jewish Question) responsible for the confiscation of Jewish property, during the Vichy regime. He carried out this task with great zeal, even before the Germans arrived in Provence. He was well known for his virulent anti-Semitic sentiments. Never mind," she concluded, "it's sweet revenge – you living in this house. He must be turning over in his grave."

We stood in front of the obelisk, in appropriate silence (even the dogs sort of paid their respects) and Suzanne gazed through her red frames at the inscriptions. "Bonjour *Monseiur* Séguret," she whispered. I kind of gazed into the distance.

Upon return to the house, I offered Suzanne a glass of rosé which she accepted gratefully. And then another, and another and another. Refusing our offer to drive her to the bus, she wandered off down the road, hair blowing in the wind and murmuring to herself. Six months later, we received a copy of the book, incredibly researched, extremely well written and totally devoid of any emotional content.

The house seems to attract attention from the heavens. Our wonderful real estate agent who sold us this house is also gazing down with pleasure from above. A few years after we came to live here permanently, as he had predicted, his son entered the agency. But unfortunately, *Monsieur* Thierry died rather suddenly shortly after.

We felt sorry but thought no more about it until my grandson, Yannick who lives in Aix, asked if he could bring a friend with him for the weekend chez nous. Since adolescents alone can be tiring unless you are ready to sit in front of an X-box with them, I readily agreed. "You don't have to pick us up," Yannick told me over the phone. (My grandson eschews public transportation whenever possible.) Jean-Baptiste's father will bring us. What a name – brings visions of a head on a platter to me.

Jean-Baptiste's father turned out to be the son of *Monsieur* Thierry. I know coincidences occur all the time, but this was pretty strong. That the grandson of

Monsieur Thierry and my grandson should become bosom pals was incredible. Neither of the boys had even been born when we bought the house. Not only were the kids pals but the young *Monsieur* Thierry and my son Jay were also friends.

This was such a remarkable chain of events that I decided to give up some offers to the gods. I invited Jean-Baptiste's parents (his mother has an incredibly chic fashion shop in Aix), his grandmother (*Monsieur* Thierry's wife of *bouillabaisse* fame), and his great-grandmother.

The last time I had seen *Madame* Thierry was the day after the sale had been completed. I had asked her and her husband to come have a glass of champagne with us at our new, but bare house, to celebrate the successful end of a very long and difficult path. I remember very clearly her looking around sipping the champagne out of a paper cup and saying: *"Vous êtes trés courageux"* (You are very courageous.)

Now some 15 years later, the house had certainly changed. This time we drank out of crystal champagne glasses and ate canapés with *foie gras,* in a well-tempered garden on comfortable wicker chairs. As we clicked glasses, she looked up. "Could you ever have imagined this, cherie," she said, raising her glass to the heavens. And then to me, "He is so happy to know how beautiful the house has become, but that our grandchildren are friends is even more important to him."

To my own surprise, since sentimentality is not one of my major traits, I lifted my glass and murmured, "Thank you *Monsieur* Thierry."

We went on to drink lots more champagne while recounting the travails of buying the house. *Monsieur* Thierry and *Madame* Boulet had a very special relationship. Maybe because he too grew grapes. He knew her weaknesses but respected her strength and she knew how to charm him. He got the house for us more or less on our terms by the old carrot and stick method. *Madame* Thierry told me he never doubted for a moment that the house would be ours.

CHAPTER 2

TENNIS ANYONE?

After J and I had spent an excruciating year rebuilding the house with all creature comforts, landscaping the huge overgrown area which had perhaps once been a garden and putting in an Olympic-sized (well almost) swimming pool, our oldest son remarked "Very nice but something is missing." Aside from the huge amount which had disappeared from our bank account, I couldn't imagine what.

"A tennis court," he announced coolly. A tennis court! One's own swimming pool was already something unimaginable for us, having grown up very happy to be able to pay the entrance to the city pool in suburban New Jersey.

But a tennis court – this was the world of "The Great Gatsby". "Relax," said Mark, "I'll pay half." Considering that he and his wife were not major tennis players, the children as yet not at all, and J had played his last match approximately 40 years ago. As for me the idea of a ball flying at the speed of sound in my direction was absolutely terrifying. I thought this a rather daring proposal. But never look a gift tennis in the court

Since the closest I have been to a tennis court was in front of the TV screen watching the US Open, Mark took over the technical details, found a constructor of tennis courts, determined exactly where it should be placed (Not where I can see it without expressly looking for it, was my one inalterable request), negotiated the cost and date of completion both of which were nearly doubled, and then vanished back to his own home on the Costa de Sol in Spain

A few weeks later, a lovely field blooming with spring wild flowers was turned into a major disaster zone. Two bulldozers dug a huge pit dumping the earth, creating hills where there were none, flattening out areas, where cherry trees bloomed, and generally creating havoc normally caused by natural catastrophes. And every day *Monsieur* Gentile (literally Mr. Nice) came by to assure me this would be the most beautiful tennis court in Provence. Where else was there such a view – the Sainte Victoire on one side, Mount Olympe and Mount Aurealien on the other? All this with the obligatory glass of Pastis and olives from Nyons, very expensive, but necessary for the true enjoyment of the yellow ambrosia.

What sounded very dreamy soon turned into a nightmare. It rained! The hill of earth became liquid mud cascading into the tennis hole. Bulldozers sank. Nobody turned up for weeks after the torrents stopped. Mr. Nice was unreachable, undoubtedly on another job. And then – voila! The whole crew was back. Engines hummed, Mr. Nice arrived each day to admire his progress and drink his pastis (cheap olives from then on) and suddenly there was a tennis court, albeit three months later than planned and don't ask the increase in price, due to, as Mr. Nice so aptly described, "unforeseen difficulties."

The court was there, complete with a pristine high referee's chair, two white benches for prospective spectators and a key attached to a miniature racket. What was not, were any sort of amenities around it, like for instance some grass. Plunked down in the middle of raw earth, bordered on one side by an enormous pile of dirt and on the other by some uprooted trees it was not exactly, to quote Mr. Nice, "he most beautiful tennis in Provence."

When I phoned Mark to ask what he had arranged for landscaping, he replied with great surprise. "Oh, that's up to you. You're the artist in the family!" With no choice and not too much help from J who was submerged in writing "an extremely important book" requiring total concentration and a tranquil environment, I steeled myself to dealing with various people experienced in moving mounds of earth, planting grass, pruning what was left of the fruit trees and installing an automatic watering system without which no lawn can survive in Provence. This feat took longer than building the tennis court itself. It was accomplished with screaming interspersed with cajoling, gallons of pastis and tons of olives. But when Mark and family arrived the next summer, there it was – the most beautiful tennis court in Provence.

We invited all the workers who had produced this miracle for a drink and a simple supper. Mark inaugurated the court by slamming the first ball to his father, which J missed to his great consternation. Mr. Nice made an elaborate toast, praising friendship and the joys of working for such great people. So, I guess the pastis and olives did the trick. The garden crew were a bit less flowery. Their chief told J he was married to a *"femme tres forte"* (very strong woman). I'm not sure this was meant as a compliment.

Now that the tennis was in place, we needed a tennis pro to teach our children and theirs the art of the game. By asking in the local sports shop, Mark found one. And that is how Victor came into our lives over 10 years ago. Short, wiry with a stand-up brush of grey hair, he has become our friend, our mentor, our source of information on everything from computers to roses.

His supply of contacts ranges from someone to fix a leaky faucet to the mayor of the village. He knows the best painter, the only reliable electrician, the local bartender who prunes cypresses into obelisks in his free time, the seller of the best tomato plants at the market, who to call to cut down a dead tree, where to buy a second-hand car. After 40 years of early morning coffee in the local café, Victor knows everyone, and everyone knows Victor. Recently he rushed off after tennis to collect some freshly caught fish from one of his coffee drinking buddies.

He has stolen the hearts of our five grandchildren and taught them the art of the game with the patience befitting a saint, weathering the moments when the two youngest were more interested in slugging each other with their rackets or the oldest stormed off the court, flinging his racket to the ground in perfect McEnroe style. Our son, Mark, his wife Françoise, Jay, the second son and Jacky, our daughter's husband spent summers perfecting their game. The other women in the family, me definitely included, preferred the white benches or better still a glass of rosé in the shade.

Ever since we arrived in the house as permanent residents instead of casual visitors, Tuesday and Thursday mornings, summer and winter, J and Victor play tennis or more correctly Victor makes the supreme effort to improve J's game. Until now, Roger Federer has nothing to fear. Victor is also retired,10 years younger than J, and in top condition from a lifetime of tennis. When J complains about a pain in his arm or a sore knee, Victor has no sympathy. "What are you, a *tamalous?"* *"Tu as mal ou?"* (Where does it hurt now?) This is a typical Provencal saying for the over 70 crowd. J did not appreciate being so categorized, but at least he now keeps his aches and pains to himself. In any case, it's better than being a *"quické mort"* (*Qui est mort* -who's dead!), a term for the 80-year-olds, reflecting their discussions at the Wednesday market.

Born in Sicily, Victor arrived in our small village at the age of nine and has never lived anywhere else. His father with the peasant's inherent love of land, bought a large piece of property and, as time went by, built houses for all his children. Married to a beautiful girl from Bretagne, a very odd but happy match, Victor lives in one of these houses surrounded by those of his brothers and sister. He has remained very, very Italian –macho, elegant and charming, albeit no nonsense. He speaks Provençal accented French, spiced up with a Sicilian tang.

There is a ritual to these tennis sessions with J. Victor arrives 15 minutes beforehand, impeccably clad in a white jogging suit or shorts in the summer, for an expresso made exactly as it would be in an Italian stand up bar. A small cup, barely half filled, with two sugar cubes. One drop over the designated amount and I drink it. With the next cup, I am extremely cautious. J is forbidden to make Victor's coffee since he has the tendency to fill any vessel to the brim and then some.

Upon Victor's arrival, our largest dog, Alias, starts to go crazy. She knows it's tennis time. The pleasure of racing around outside the tennis court hundreds of times is one of her favorite doggy pleasures inextricably connected to Victor. Just the sight of a tennis racket sets her off. Victor barricades himself with chairs to avoid the drooling muzzle and muddy paws on his pristine whites. *"Arret"* (Stop – go away) he yells, endearing himself to her even more. We have not been able to convince him to dress in black when coming to us.

One of the highlights of summer is being invited to Victor's for pizza, en masse –kids, grand kids, friends. I have eaten pizza all over the world from New York's pepperoni, sausage and stringy mozzarella, crunchy crusted pie at Ray's Pizza to Mama Mia's in Naples. Nothing but nothing holds a candle to the master's. The tomato sauce is home made by Danielle from the zillion plants in the garden.

She once told me very discreetly in keeping with her character: "This is the last year! If Victor wants sauce, he can make it himself!" The outburst, if you can attribute such a word to Danielle, came after 8 hours a day for a week peeling, seeding, boiling, straining and bottling tomatoes.

One meets all kinds of people at the long table in Victor's garden – rich Parisians with a summer house in the region, the local plumber, a young ballet dancer whose parents are Victor's friends, the olive guy from the market as well as the mayor, not only of our village but the adjoining one

Neither Victor nor Danielle drink wine, making do with cider. When I pointed out that cider also contains some alcohol, he gave the typical shrug. "Not enough to make a difference." But he sure knows how to pick wines. His knowledge is broad, and he buys with his ears, following the advice of various wine merchants. Some of the best wines we have drunk here were those accompanied by the humble pizza.

Victor has tried to convince me that making pizza dough is the easiest thing in the world. Maybe it is if you happen to be Sicilian. Mine becomes either sticky, hard, mushy, tasteless and sometimes plain disgusting. So one morning after tennis Victor decided to teach me the art. Armed with flour, yeast, my bowl, salt and olive oil, he proceeded to whip up 10 perfectly equal balls of pizza dough in 10 minutes, which were left to rise while we had a leisurely lunch.

Admittedly I still had a lot of trouble getting those balls into a suitable pizza pan. My pastry rolling skills are somewhat lacking, but at least the finished crust was delicious.

Clothes are his mania. Victor collects them like one collects paintings or stamps. Danielle, his wife, complains of lack of closet space for her. There are dozens of shirts never worn, most still in their original packing, pants in every color imaginable and then sometimes in duplicate, a top brand range of tennis attire and running suits, not to mention jackets of every sort and material. *"C"etait en solde et le vendeur m"a donné encore une remise"* (It was on sale and the salesman gave me an additional discount) he proudly boasts after each new acquisition. Arriving in a very chic grey jogging suit and matching sweater, he announced that he would have to leave exactly on time, "There's a sale at Gago, he explained, (a very chic men's shop in Aix-en Provence). I already bought 6 pairs of pants and 6 tee-shirts but there is a jacket I really want. The salesgirl likes me. She said she would give me another 20% off the sale price "

Everyone likes a bargain, but Victor pulled off the deal of the year. His passions run deeper than just clothes. Victor has lusted after a Mercedes SL convertible for years. Finally finding one via the Internet, second-hand and for a reasonable price, in

Montpelier, about 200 kilometers from our village, he made an appointment to go check it out. Drinking his ritual morning coffee with his usual café cronies, he announced his intention to buy this incredible car. "Hmph" snorted one of his companions, "why go to Montpelier? There's one right here at Ferretti's garage." Victor gulped down the last dregs of his coffee and rushed over.

The garage is run by two brothers, Guy in charge of sales and Denis of repairs. As luck would have it, Guy, the more commercial of the two, was on vacation. "No problem," said Denis whose interest is in the mechanics of cars, not selling them, "here is the name and telephone number of the owner." Within an hour Victor and the Mercedes' owner were in deep discussion.

"*Trés belle voiture*" (beautiful car), said Victor longingly, "but much too expensive for me."

"I think actually it is quite a good price," countered the owner.

"*Mais bien sùr,*" (absolutely) nodded Victor, "but I am retired and not very rich." With a bit of discussion and lot of Victorian charm, the price went down another 2000 euros.

"*Vous est très amable,*" (you are very nice) but it is still too much for me."

"You too are very nice, so I would really like you to have the car. I just came back from a year in the United States and I bought a new car and that's why I am selling this one."

"Oh," said Victor, "I have a cousin in America, in New York state, in Saratoga."

"What"! That's where I lived," exclaimed Mr. Mercedes.

"My cousin has a pizzeria, "Stromboli." Do you know it?" Victor asked.

"Know it? I ate there every week. Best pizza in town. Vinnie is my amigo. He's your cousin? Tell me what you want to pay for the car and it's yours. "

"Well," said Victor trying to look very embarrassed instead of delighted, "I could manage 10,000 euros."

"Deal!" replied the ex-owner, giving Victor a huge hug.

Needless to say, Guy was not pleased to find out the car sold for half the asking price. Denis must have been the target of extreme brotherly fury. Victor did assure Guy, though, that he would bring the car to his garage for maintenance.

Victor dreams of visiting his cousin in New York, where to quote Victor, he has the best pizzeria in the U. S Almost as good as the cousins in Sicily. And more than anything he wants us to accompany him. I've tried to explain to him that Saratoga is not exactly near Manhattan. Again, the shrug. Nothing is ever a problem for him. "We'll first stay with my cousin, eat real Italian food and then you can take us to New York." Danielle is terrified of flying and will only consider going with us and a box of tranquilizers. Victor also has trepidations about not speaking English, although we have explained to him that probably half of New York speaks Italian. His command of the German language is equally non-existent but, on a trip to Dresden, he managed quite well to avoid what he most hates with two words, "*Keine schlager*." (No cream) Another of his quirks.

Although we haven't yet attained the Gatsby way of life, our tennis court has given us a certain status. Maybe everyone coming over to play is not in white flowing skirts or impeccable flannels, but the social life around it has very much enriched us. Especially when friends come bearing not only rackets but great wine.

CHAPTER 3

FOOD FOR THOUGHT
(AND THE WINE TO GO WITH IT)

TRUFFES
1000€ / Kg

After the weather, food is probably the most popular topic of conversation in France, nowhere more so than in Provence. Next comes wine. Or maybe it is the other way around. It may be the only country in the world where the farmer's wife can whip up a gourmet *paté de foie gras,* and the farmer will know exactly what wine to drink with it.

Dinner party discussions revolve around what one is eating, drinking, advice on how one of the guest's great grandmothers prepared the same dish, what one ate yesterday, the new chef at the local restaurant, the appalling lack of a good cheese shop in the village, the excellent rosé at one of the nearby vineyards and the lousy white at another. Politics, business, and money being taboo, one would think food and wine were safe subjects.

Ah but non! Passionate debates on what Bourgogne one should use in a daube Provençal (beef stew) version of *bœuf Bourguinon* have been known to end up in blows, but I think this is a bit of French folklore. Talking about soufflés may make tempers rise as high as this delicacy. The drinking of a glass of wine can set off an hour's round table of opinions. The expertness with which not only men, but the women too, discuss this staple of French life never ceases to amaze me.

Manners at a French dinner party don't count for much by Dutch (who have the ridiculous habit of eating a slice of bread and cheese with a knife and fork) or American standards. A bread and butter plate or waiting until everyone has been served before raising your own fork is not the French way. Bread is broken on the table, resulting in millions of crumbs, food is downed the minute it is put on your plate and no real Frenchman waits to try the wine – sniffing it, sloshing it around and drinking, without regard to his neighbor who may still have an empty glass. But this natural approach is inbred in a people who have such an important culture of food and wine. Enjoyment is the top priority. Who wants to eat their *gigot* (roast leg of lamb) cold, waiting for 10 other people to get their portion.

"Bon appetit" before beginning a meal is considered very bourgeois and "not done." Toasts are also not *de rigeur* either, unless someone is having his 100th birthday party. And never, but never, "Cheers," *"Proost,"* "Down the Hatch," *"L'Chaim,"* "Here's mud in your eye," or any other colorful wish to your fellow guests. Glass clinking is regarded as archaic. Having noted this – in less exalted circles people do say *"Salut,"* and give a friendly tap to your glass

Dinner parties are one thing. Lunch is another world, especially here in the South where the sky is blue, the sun shines, the light shimmers and time has no meaning. A typical Provençal Sunday repast lasts about 5 hours but can be longer in summer. We are quite famous for our *"dejeuners d'éte"* (summer lunches), nothing to do with my quasi French, American, Chinese cuisine but for the huge *platanes* shading our enormous graveled terrace.

On a hot July afternoon, I could serve bread and water, and no one would complain, sitting in the cool shade of the trees, gazing at the Montagne Sainte Victoire and listening to the *cigalles* (cicadas). Of course, I don't. We drink champagne and rosé, eat cold gazpacho with spicy shrimp and octopus, barbecued dorade and big fat stuffed tomatoes which I can never believe really grew in my garden.

There's an array of cheese, not from our village, but from the market in Aix. My favorite is a creamy St. Felicien which is probably 100% milk fat and could give a real zing to anyone's cholesterol. For dessert, huge deep red strawberries from Carpentras, a town which has the monopoly on the best strawberries in the region. Strawberries, despite heroic efforts of our guardien, refuse to grow *chez nous*.

Food markets herald the seasons in Provence. White and yellow peaches, sweet orange melons from

47

Cavaillon, mean summer. Asparagus and strawberries are to be eaten when the sun is high. Like everywhere in the western world, you can have cherries in December, mangoes all year, melons in the winter but I cannot get used to this. It's like drinking pastis in New York.

In Autumn, huge pumpkins appear everywhere. Mine are turned into soup made with coconut milk or in chunks roasted with olive oil and garlic. There's squash in gorgeous fall colors, celeriac, leek, big orange carrots, cabbages in all shapes and hues, a variety of apples from green to yellow to rose and deep carmine, bright orange tangerines from Corsica, with their green leaves still attached. Ah – and the grapes. At the time of the *vendange* (harvesting the wine grapes), market stalls are top heavy with green and deep purple specimens. They all have pits. I have never discovered how in the United States they grow grapes without them.

The variety of mushrooms is hallucinating, and local legend has it that if you pick and eat the wrong ones you can hallucinate into your grave. *Cepes, girolles, sanguine, pleurotte,* (*pleurer* means to cry in French and I wonder if these are weeping mushrooms). Admittedly, none of these come cheap but as I tell J, "filet mignon is expensive too." I have learned you never wash wild mushrooms, just gently brush off the earth and then into a pan of hot olive oil with some garlic, parsley and ground black pepper. Only salt them when they are seared, otherwise they get watery. Eat immediately.

We have an assortment of mushrooms sprouting all over the property like you wouldn't believe. All sizes, shapes and colors but probably not edible. My grandson, Andrew, and I once gathered baskets full and brought them to the local pharmacy, which is supposed to be able to recognize which are poisonous. The pharmacist gave us a blank look. "Why don't you look it up on Google?" she suggested. So much for that bit of French village lore.

A weathered peasant, leaning heavily on his cane, patiently waiting his turn to discuss his various ailments, came over, sniffed our treasures with the disdain of years of experience selecting mushrooms. "*Tous, c'est la merde,* (It's all shit)" he declared. After that sanguine appraisal, Andrew decided to take them to school for a kind of show and tell. I wonder if he told it as it was.

From the first of November on, stands pop up all over the villages, hawking (and shucking) oysters. Thank heaven for the last since J has not managed to master this art. Often driving home from Aix early in the evening, we stop at our favorite oyster vendor and pick up two dozen. Oysters, dark bread, a juicy lemon and a glass of white wine from the chateau next door makes cooking dinner totally superfluous. Sometimes I feel very decadent. Oysters were a delicacy one ate on special occasions, expensive and chic. Sitting in front of the TV casually devouring oysters we bought on the way home is something else. But it is the French way.

Oysters, *foie gras,* and truffles are not considered extravagant food choices in the weeks before, during and after Christmas. Every self-respecting French woman knows how to prepare *foie gras,* . Give her the whole goose or duck liver and in no time, she has prepared *paté de foie gras,* aux truffes, with cognac, *en croute*, in a terrine with oranges and figs, or just pure with fleur de sel.

For me it is still an unattainable goal although my *gardien* says a 4-year-old child can do it. Certainly, only a French one. My son, Jay, who lives in Aix-en-Provence, lightly fries up slices of raw *foie gras,* and wraps it in pastry dough, served with a confit of fresh figs. His cooking talents must derive from some unknown French ancestor, certainly not from his father whose only kitchen skill is to *fatiguez* (toss) the salade. I content myself, and my guests, with the paté de *foie gras,* offered by the local supermarket. Make no mistake, the most modest of supermarkets offer a variety of *foie gras,* which would make Harrods food manager blush.

Behind the counter of our local supermarket, there is a young girl who looks thirteen and can tell you everything you ever wanted to know about *foie gras.* Either duck or goose, *mi-cuit* (half cooked) *cuit au torchon* (wrapped in a sort of dish towel), where it came from – les Landes, Perigord, Alsace, le Gers, which is the best quality for the price and a recommendation for a confit of onions to go with it. Only in France!

On the Sunday before Christmas, the small village of Rognes quite near us holds its *foire des truffes* (truffle fair). Provence produces three-quarters of the black truffles in France. It's not for nothing that they are called the *diamant noir* (black diamond). The prices are astronomical, and you probably could get a small diamond ring for the same amount as a kilo of truffles. The good news is that you don't need very much for a taste thrill. Expensive or not, the market is jam packed and not with lookers. Business is brisk with savvy buyers, rubbing a truffle between their palms to make sure the aroma is persistent, the sign of a true truffle. If you are not a truffle lover, the odor might asphyxiate you.

My first experience with the black diamond was lunch at a very chic couple's house. The starter course was *brouillades aux truffes* (scrambled eggs with truffles). The taste of truffles will always be associated with the unwelcome hand of my host on my thigh. Jean-Philippe was known for his touchy, feely ways preferably practiced on young ladies. Although harmless, all of our friends" daughters, and mine as well, absolutely refused to be seated next to him. I was the next best choice.

I listened attentively as he explained the special qualities of these particular truffles, their origin, their price, while stroking my thigh. Looking deeply into his eyes I told him if he didn't get his hand off me pronto, I would dump my whole plate of black diamonds right in his lap. With superb French aplomb, he replied, "Ah, but you are much more beautiful than truffles. I just couldn't resist your charms." Well, I must admit this isn't a scenario that plays often in my life.

Maybe this helped develop my taste for truffles! When the restaurants start serving this specialty, beginning in December, although the truffle is at its best in February, I never pass it by. I also like the Italian style. The waiter stands over your plate of hot, very thin spaghetti and grates away. If you get distracted during the session you can easily down a 100 Euro pasta.

The French eat some strange things, which do not pass easily into an Anglo-Saxon stomach. Tripe, brains, heart (I used to feed this to a dog I once had. Made him terribly aggressive) kidneys, lungs, blood sausages, frogs legs and snails. Snails are the most acceptable since they are usually drowned in lots of butter and garlic. So, if you forget the slimy connotation, they are really not too bad.

Sometimes, no matter how much one tries to assimilate, it doesn't work. We were invited for dinner at friends in their wonderful mas (typical farmhouse in Southern France) that had been in the family forever. Roaring fireplace, comfortable chairs, table beautifully set with the family silver, a magnificent centerpiece of roses from the garden, all very elegant but at the same time informal and very country. The first course, typically Provençal, was grilled red peppers in olive oil and garlic, a *tapenade* (sort of puree) of anchovies and olives, marinated eggplant slices, tiny tomatoes stuffed with goat cheese and a wonderful bread baked by our hostess. The red wine from their own vineyards was a perfect accompaniment. And then the main course arrived. "I've made you something really special, very Provencal," announced Danielle, our hostess, *pied paquet.* It's really a lot of work but I knew you would love it."

Unfortunately, I knew what *pied paquet* was, pig's intestines stuffed with some other unspeakable parts of the animal. J, who has no real knowledge of food and eats anything, dug in with gusto. "Delicious," he pronounced. I did my best. Took one bite. It wasn't so much the taste as the texture. Just the way you imagine the lining of an intestine, very, very slippery. I pushed it around my plate a bit, eating the vegetables around it and trying not to obviously choke. My tablemate regarded his plate and then me. "Dan," he cried, "How could you! I never eat this. It's disgusting." With that he pushed his plate away. Being French and her cousin, I guess he didn't feel any compunction expressing his opinion. He turned to me," Don't eat it. You'll get sick." J finished his plate and took seconds. On the way home, I told him what he had eaten. "So?" he replied. It was really good."

Our friend Elizabeth, married to a French diplomat, is absolutely the high priestess of Provençal entertaining. Their house, built by Christian's father, mostly from World War 11 surplus materials, looks as if it has been there since the 18th century. Facing the Sainte Victoire and surrounded by vineyards, it epitomizes everything wonderful about Provence. A fire in 1989 which raged on the mountain reducing the landscape to a charred nether world, descended onto their property, burning their trees, bushes and almost reaching the house. We came a few days later to see what we could do to help and found them, the house and the garden black, covered in soot. But discouraged? Absolutely not, only grateful that they were able to save the house. "Well," said Christian with incredible optimism, "our view has changed. It is more open." I think I would have run away screaming, never to return.

They planted new trees – a line of cypresses, now ten years later, high and proud, and *chêne truffier* (special oak trees which encourage truffles to grow beneath them, most probably in 50 years judging by their size when they were planted), changed the configuration of the garden to keep the new view and repainted the outside of the house a wonderful shade of off-white, unusual here in Provence. Maybe to put behind them forever, the blackness of the fire. It is their family home inherited from Christian's father and will be passed down to their children, hopefully with lots of truffles. Never, never did they even consider giving it up.

Elizabeth is not only an incredible cook but a natural decorator. The house, which could be a photo reportage in any magazine on Provence, is full of wonderful things. Beautiful antique closets, chests, tables, portraits of ancestors – all inherited- but also Polish pottery, Japanese artefacts and modern paintings acquired from all the countries in which Christian has been posted. There is just enough shabbiness, a crack in the wall here, a ceiling shedding plaster, a couch with the fabric worn, shutters awaiting a paint job to give the house the true soul of its occupants.

Elizabeth is equally at ease catering a dinner for 200 people, which she did for her son's wedding or whipping up an *aioli* for eight. *Aioli* is a garlic mayonnaise, made by crushing garlic, olive oil and raw egg with a mortar and pestle until it reaches exactly the right consistency. You need to lift weights for years to acquire the muscles to do this. It is the reason to eat boiled vegetables – carrots, leeks, celery, potatoes – and boiled fish and drink a lot of rosé to weaken the effect of the garlic. A siesta is imperative after this meal.

I learned from Elizabeth the effect of decorating on a large scale. No small basket of fruit on her dining room table. A huge cornucopia of kilos of tomatoes spilling over. One pumpkin? Never, at least 10. Fruits and vegetables in enormous quantities replace bouquets of flowers. Bare branches reaching almost to the ceiling are winter floral arrangements. I asked her once "What do you do with all the tomatoes."

"What do you do with a dead bouquet?" she replied. The tomatoes cost a lot less and are turned into tomato soup, tomato puree, tomato sauce, even tomato jam – all canned or frozen for winter consumption when tomatoes are not up to snuff. I have to admit I now use broccoli, eggplant, peppers, zucchini and sometimes even string beans for table decoration. When complimented on my originality, J says I should just say "thank you." But I am too honest and give the credit where it belongs. Although I must say, modestly, I have kind of gilded the basics with my own ingenuity.

Elizabeth came for lunch recently and naturally I felt a competitive sensation arising. It was a "simple meal," a *pintade* (guinea fowl) sitting on a bed of sauerkraut, accompanied by small potatoes with rosemary, pear chutney, (yes, made by me from the zillions of pears falling from our two pear trees) a great local wine and a brie which ran off the plate (right into our dog Alias" mouth when I left it on the kitchen counter, fortunately after lunch) Actually she never steals but such a great smelly cheese was too hard to resist. . She doesn't even have to jump up to reach it but just puts her head on the counter and calmly laps it up.

Needless to say, when Elizabeth kept murmuring "delicious," I preened. So here is the recipe for success:

You buy a really good *pintade*, fill the cavity with about 6 cloves of peeled garlic. You can put some between the wings and the legs where they are attached to the rest of the bird, throw a bit of olive oil over it and add a tiny bit of water at the bottom of the casserole. Cover. Put in a slow oven and cook, basting now and then. Mix some black and red pepper grains through the ready cooked sauerkraut, which comes from the supermarket. Stick it in the microwave a few minutes to heat up and put in the pan with the *pintade* for the last 15 minutes. Since I am very bad at following recipes, you will just have to use the taste, look and feel method.

Potatoes with rosemary are one of my favorite recipes since it does not involve peeling, mashing, frying or any other complicated operations. Take very small potatoes, cut them in half. Pour some good olive oil into a shallow baking dish, turn the potatoes around in the oil and place cut side up. Put in lots of fresh rosemary branches and sprinkle with sea salt. Put in the oven with the *pintade*.

When they start to look a little dry, put them face down in the olive oil. It's the rosemary and all that garlic that makes it Provençal – at least that's what you tell your guests. If chutney is not your thing, just fry up some thinly sliced onions (use the robot unless you enjoy weeping) mix with a little honey, some salt and lemon juice.

Actually, Elizabeth's recipes are not very much more detailed. She is definitely experimental and never worries about quantities – a teaspoon, a tablespoon, 2 ounces or 6 ounces. It doesn't really make all that much difference. Or so she claims. She is extremely generous with her advice. Take mayonnaise, for example. Every self-respecting French woman can fabricate a perfect mayonnaise, creamy and totally together, in the time it takes me to measure out the oil. I have watched the process, have read about it, even bought a book on how to correct cooking disasters but, nevertheless, all my attempts at mayonnaise end up divided – the oil on top, the rest on the bottom. "But it is so simple," she tells me, "even a child (children really can do amazing things in France) can make it," as she again explains the technique.

Pie crusts are another thing. "Two minutes work," claims Elizabeth, "just mix the ingredients, let it rest a bit and then press the dough into the pie plate with your fingers." Yeah right! Mine is either full of lumps or holes. I have discovered an incredible ready-made pie crust which is infallible. You just carefully ꜱᵤₚ the protective wax paper from under the pie before you serve, put it on a great plate and who will know. Don't ask, don't tell.

Elizabeth graciously agreed to give me her secret recipes – fast and delicious. I happily pass these on to you, dear reader. Remember it's child's play.

PATÉ DE FOIES DE VOLAILLE

(Provençal version of chopped liver)

Poach chicken livers in white wine, salt, pepper, bay leaves, and thyme until there is no trace of blood. Drain the livers in a colander. Put in the blender with half their weight in softened butter, crushed juniper berries, salt, pepper and a small glass of gin (my grandmother never put that in her chopped liver!) and mix. Place in a nice terrine and refrigerate for a least two hours before serving. Can be a starter or hors d'oeurvre served on toast.

PÂTÉ DE SARDINES

Another paté even easier, bound to elicit cries of "What's in it!" is Elizabeth's *Pâté de Sardines à la desprogienne, humblement.* Pierre Desproges was a journalist/humorist who loved not only good food and wine, but his theory was that sometimes one is allowed to prefer opening a can, eat directly out of it while drinking wine from a plastic bottle, sitting on a broken chair. "His sense of humor still inspires me," explained Elizabeth. "He died in 1986 leaving this recipe which I keep making as an homage to him."

He named it this way, à la *desprogienne, humblement,* kind of like Woody Allen saying, "excuse me for everything."

250 grams of sardines (canned, whole and in oil, bones and all)

250 grams softened butter

75 grams of double concentrated tomato purée

1 shallot cut up

Then add whatever you like – salt, pepper, tabasco, hot red pepper, fennel seeds but most important a few drops of pastis!

Mix it all in the blender, arrange in a terrine and refrigerate for at least an hour. Serve with chunks of really good bread.

Ratatouille is a well-known Provençal dish made with summer vegetables – tomatoes, eggplant, zucchini, onions and red and green peppers. Elizabeth's "tian" is faster, easier and more delicious.

TIAN D'AUBERGINE
3 beautiful *aubergine* (eggplant)

6 white onions

3 peppers (green, red and orange)

olive oil (lots and good quality)

In a big round earthenware casserole pour in 2 tablespoons of olive oil.

Place a layer of onions, coarsely chopped, a layer of *aubergine* (do not peel) cut in pieces

Pour on some olive oil, salt and pepper

Add a layer of peppers (no seeds please) cut in pieces

More olive oil, salt and pepper.

And so on, ending with a layer of onions.

Pour on some more olive oil, salt and pepper.

Put in a very slow oven and cook for 3 hours.

Hot or cold, it is fantastic.

BOUILLABAISSE

Bouillabaisse is the visiting card of Marseille. Originally a poor man's dish made by fisherman from fish too undesirable to sell to restaurants or on the market, it has now become one of the most expensive meals you can have in Marseille, that is if you want the real thing.

Elizabeth's version has no pretensions. It is a *soupe de poisons* (fish soup) but as delicious as any bouillabaisse I have ever eaten and paid a fortune for. It also has the wonderful advantage of being easy to make and cheap.

Sauté 3 large chopped onions in olive oil. Put in some grains of fennel, 3 cut up tomatoes and a few thinly sliced potatoes on top. Cover over with water. Add, salt, pepper, a good dash of saffron and a few branches of fennel. Simmer slowly for 10 or 15 minutes in a covered pot until the potatoes are cooked. You can do this in advance. Just before serving bring to a slow boil and throw in whatever kind of white fish you have around in whatever quantity you like. Cook for another 5 or 10 minutes, grind some pepper over the whole soup and serve with rouille.

Ah, *rouille*! That's what gives a classic and not so classic *bouillabaisse* zing. Normally a process involving a mortar and pestle to smash the garlic, blend in the oil drop by drop incorporating some bread crumbs and chili peppers, requiring arm muscles developed by daily weight lifting. The alternative is to combine 3 peeled cloves of garlic, 1 teaspoon of hot red pepper, a handful of white bread soaked and wrung out. Put in the blender and mix while drizzling 3 tablespoons of olive oil and one tablespoon of soup until it looks like mayonnaise.

Serve the soup boiling hot with lots of fish, potatoes and tomatoes. Top with *croutons* and pass the *rouille*. Leave your guests time for a nap.

D'AGNEAU CONFITE

If you are like me and dread making dishes involving last minute cooking, which usually end up being overdone, raw, or burnt, Elizabeth's *Epaule d"Agneau Confite* (slow cooked shoulder of lamb) is a fail-safe recipe.

Pour a bit olive oil into a casserole – either earthenware or cast iron. Add chopped onions, a boned lamb shoulder and lots of spices – rosemary, thyme, bay leaves or oriental spices – coriander, cumin, garam-marsala, salt and pepper and whatever else you like. If you are a lot of people add a second shoulder on top of the first, cover with lots of chopped onions, again salt, pepper and spices. Cover tightly and place in the oven (2 for gas). Just leave it for three hours. If you like, take a peek now and then but Elizabeth assures me even if you don't, it comes out perfectly.

Christian, Elizabeth's husband is an esoteric cook. He looks at the world through the eyes of a 19th century man, enjoying the many small pleasures of life, from the reflection of light in a glass of rosé wine to watching the dawn come over the Sainte Victoire.

Small details enrich his life like finding wild marjoram growing at the sides of our road. One of his hobbies is inventing recipes, preferably not too complicated but original. This one I have tried and although I cheated on the crust, it still came out quite amazingly.

QUICHE AUX CEPES

For the crust *pate brisée* (pastry crust) – I cheat and use the readymade kind. You need 250 grams of flour, 125 grams of softened butter, water, salt and mix gently. Don't insist too much. Spread it out on your pie plate. Prick with a fork. Start pre-heating your oven (5 for gas).

Beat three eggs with milk and pour onto the crust. Scatter some bacon cubes if you like over the mixture, not absolutely necessary but Christian likes it that way. Top with one or two packages of frozen *cepes*, (porcini mushrooms) without defrosting. Put in the oven for 30 minutes. Drink with a nice burgundy and toast Christian.

ROSÉ

Rosé wine and Provence are inextricably linked. It is the classic summer drink. Although the vineyards here produce red and white as well, rosé is the staple of their existence and ours too in the summer. It comes in every shade of pink - pink with an orange tint, baby girl pink, pink so dark it is almost red, purplish pink, rose petal pink, pink almost fuchsia, sunset pink.

In the light of a summer day, a glass of rosé is a table decoration. Rosé wine is the lemonade of wine lovers when the sun shines and temperatures rise. It is drunk in a totally different way than reds or whites - no sniffing, no sloshing about in the glass. For this summer wine, it is not the quality but the quantity that counts. We have been to lunches where a bottle per person is the norm. And *quelle horreur* (unbelievably awful) it is not uncommon to throw some ice cubes into your glass. Restaurants put an ice bucket on your table when you order a bottle of rosé, without even being asked! But don't be fooled, this lemonade packs a punch. The alcohol content can go up to 13. 5 degrees, well on a par with a Bordeaux or Bourgogne of which one drinks much less. The length of summer siestas are in direct relation to the amount of rosé consumed at lunch.

Most Provençals drink the wine of the region in all three colors. J and I often make the rounds of various local and not so local vineyards in search of the perfect red, white or rosé at a reasonable price, considering that our consumption is daily.

It takes a lot of patience going from one vineyard to the other and tasting lots of really terrible wine. These expeditions are better done when the weather is warm. Most of the caves are freezing cold and you can't just go in and leave after one gulp. It is an imperative form of politeness to listen as the owner talks with passion about his wine. And they all do. Every wine, great, mediocre or downright lousy, is the pride of its producer.

A friend gave us a book entitled "Wine under 10 Euros." Armed with this guide, we took a tour of all those listed more or less in our area. The most intriguing vineyard, about 20 kilometers from our house, promising a rosé of distinction, was well hidden. There was no sign and only by asking about 10 people did we finally find it.

The gate was opened by an old farmer, eyeing us very suspiciously. "You here for wine?" he asked. *"Oui, oui,"* replied J with enthusiasm.

"I'll call my son," he kind of mumbled, "but he won't sell you any. We don't sell to people we don't know. There's not enough." We had found a real boutique winemaker. The tasting room was in a converted garage.

A very handsome young man arrived. "What can I do for you," he asked with a big smile.

J, slightly intimidated, an unusual feeling for him, answered, "We'd like to buy some wine. It is so highly recommended that we have come specially."

"From America?" asked our young wine maker incredulously. We only have to say two words in French and our accent gives us away. "Oh no," said J, "we live in Provence."

"I guess my father told you, we don't make very much, and we only sell to people we know."

"Well," said J, with his best public relations manner, "now you know us."

We came away with four cases of the best rosé we had ever had for the price of Coca Cola. And indeed, now he does know us and greets us with a friendly "How many cases would you like?" This winemaker is a guarded secret. We won't tell even our best friends although we do share the wine with them. After all, how many people can he know.

CHAPTER 4

SOCIAL LIFE

There are various hubs of social life in the village and I'm not talking about courses in flower arranging, bridge or macramé, yoga, the local bodybuilding establishment or organized rambles for the golden oldies. These and many more activities jazz up the village, but appeal to special interest groups. The social events I mean are available to all regardless of sex, age, profession or political views, and what's more, free. In order of importance I rank the pharmacy number one.

Buying a box of aspirin can easily take up half the morning. Nobody just plunks down his or her prescription, pays and leaves. First of all there is the Carte Vital (literally vital card.) Since health care in France is universal, this card entitles the French to (mostly) free medicines and you must present it before any transaction takes place. Of course, the person in front of me has forgotten hers, entailing a long sorrowful plea concerning the necessity of immediate delivery of the medicine and a sworn promise to return with the card. My pharmacist is having none of it but that does not shorten the process.

Finally, after much scrunching around deep in her purse and emptying all sorts of strange things on the counter, she finds the card in her wallet in the place reserved for her grocery list. Undaunted by the long line behind her, a lengthy and involved discussion follows on how, how long and why she should take the pills. No one but me seems to mind the interminable wait. They are too busy discussing various aches and pains, the state of their varicose veins, the latest scandal about the dentist who ran off with one of his patients never to be seen again, or comparing the exalted qualities of children and grandchildren. And there are one or two chairs to relax in while waiting. I always assumed these were for people a bit weak in the legs, but I now know they are put there for the comfort of the local yentas (Yiddish, not French, for gossipers).

I discovered early on, privacy is not valued very much at some pharmacies. My dermatologist had given me a prescription for a vitamin A cream. "It will make your skin beautiful," he promised, after having burned off two ugly brown spots on my cheek. With this boost of optimism, I proffered my prescription for the cream to the pharmacist. He carefully scrutinized my face and cried out in a voice that seemed to come from a loudspeaker, "Ah, vitamin A, fantastic for all those little wrinkles. My wife uses it too."

"It doesn't help very much after a certain age," said the woman behind me, putting in her two cents as well. I left with a huge decrease in self-esteem.

This was mild compared to the experience of our gym trainer, Marie, who is shy, extremely discreet and had gotten a most embarrassing (for her) illness, hemorrhoids. The pharmacist regarded her prescription. "Hemorrhoids," he exclaimed with glee. "*Quel mahleur!*" (what a disaster)." Very painful. My brother's wife's sister-in-law was also a victim. Had to go everywhere with an inflatable tube to sit on."

Marie, who is extremely well-mannered almost to a fault, leaned over the counter and said quietly, "*Ta guelle.*" (a very rude French "shut-up")

We have both since changed pharmacies.

The girls in the new pharmacy are better trained in social graces. When I came to get our yearly vials of flu-shot vaccine and asked for the insurance form, a pretty young thing answered, "*Mais non, Madame*, the insurance only pays for those over 65." I happily forked over the 6 euros rather than admit to the awful truth.

Thanks to my housekeeper, I have also discovered the pharmacy beats an Internet dating service. Claudie is always in a hurry and has no patience for slow drivers or for slow walkers. In her rush to get out of the pharmacy, she kind of ran into a gentleman slowly limping to the door. "*Allez-y*" (go ahead), obviously you are more handicapped than I," he remarked sarcastically.

Claudie may be impatient but she is not impolite. "I'm so sorry," she apologized, "please excuse me."

Looking at her closely, he remarked "You are a beautiful woman. "

"Well, thank you," replied Claudie.

"Tell me," asked the slightly disabled but still rather handsome man, "does your husband appreciate you? Does he give you enough – you know what I mean – affection? My wife died a few years ago so I know what it means to miss a hug, a kiss and more."

"Well thank you for your concern but I am quite satisfied with my husband," replied Claudie, a bit shocked.

"Even so," he went on, "you know it is very good for *l'amour* to have a change now and then."

That did it! "*Au revoir*," retorted Claudie.

"Wait just a moment," insisted *Monsieur* the would-be lover, "if you are not interested, perhaps you have a friend." Claudie was out the door in two seconds and this time the shove was not accidental.

Running a close second is the post office. This operation is a sort of jack-of-all trades. You can send a letter in various ways, simply, registered, moderately quickly, very quickly and by slow boat. But the office also functions as a bank. Believe me these financial services are extremely time consuming which is quite normal, except one stands in the same line to buy a stamp or send money to Algeria. It can be even worse if the local café holder is in front of you counting out a thousand Euros in coins. On a good day, there are three windows open. On a bad one, you would do well to have a book with you.

The post ladies are well up on village news and their clients take advantage to hear the latest. Here again no one is impatient. There is just too much going on to get bored. Kids pushing each other to the floor, screaming with delight, their mothers too busy discussing the advantage of blonde streaked hair over red, to even notice. Nor does anyone seem to mind, except me, as I exercise formidable self-control to stop myself from giving the shrieking monsters a good smack. Then there's a young couple cooing, totally oblivious to the long wait. Two rather well-attired businessmen behind me are discussing their investments, oblivious to the axiom "time is money."

J loves the post office. He talks to everyone. Not at all hurried, he fits right into the scene happily discussing the weather or anything else that comes into his head. He has a special relationship with the blonde, well-endowed postmistress who keeps him informed of all the new stamps. I wouldn't want to be in line behind him. He claims that everyone enjoys his camaraderie and it's probably true.

His charm actually works, since he is allowed to come down to the post office to collect the The New York Times on days it doesn't arrive with the mail lady, which is a frequent occurrence. Through sleet and snow is not the motto of the French postal service. Between strikes, vacations and replacements who can't find our house, we are lucky if we get the mail 4 days out of 6.

The non-delivery of the newspaper has an upside. It gives J the chance to stop by his favorite café, of course the one Victor frequents, and chat with the guys standing around drinking a morning pastis. I can't imagine what he talks about, not being interested in either football or the lottery, the main topics of discussion, but he assures me he has very interesting conversations. Ten AM being a little early for pastis he always orders *un café allongé* (a coffee with lots of hot water added). "Too early for *allongé*," laughs the blonde buxom owner, taking the literal meaning of the word, stretched out.

J came home one day after a coffee visit with a most remarkable story. The man seated at the table next to him ordered a beer. Nothing unusual, except he also ordered one (in a small glass bowl) for his dog, a Yorkshire terrier. The two beers were set down on the table. From the elevated position on his master's lap, the canine client leisurely sipped his beer, pausing now and then to look around. I accused J of a pastis induced fantasy but had to apologize a few weeks later when I saw the beer drinkers enjoying their pint on the sunny café terrace.

J also has a connection with the local garage since his acquaintance with his car doesn't go past putting the key in the ignition. He goes to the garage to have the tires pumped up, to check the oil, to have the clock changed from summer to winter time and a myriad of other things, which anyone else would be too embarrassed to ask a mechanic to do. He also is often there for the various wounds inflicted on the auto when backing into the low sneaky poles put everywhere in Aix.

Denis, the garage owner, two heads smaller than J and very thin and wiry, looks up from under the car he's working on. "Hey Osama," (the common attribute with Osama bin Laden is J's beard) "what's new in the terrorism world."

J looks in the other direction. "Anyone seen Denis," he asks. This is the absolute standard repartee. But sometimes there are variations. Once, when walking into the garage with the usual "Where's Denis?" question, a rather old and somewhat toothless man standing next to a battered pick-up truck, replied laconically, "In jail. He raped the pharmacist."

Denis shrugged his shoulders. "He's just jealous." You have to know that the lady in the pharmacy is about 6 feet tall and weighs probably 200 pounds.

Without so much as a grin, the guy turned to J and said, "*C'est vrai!*" (It's true), got into his pick-up and drove out of the garage. Some sense of humor. Now when Denis greets him with "Osama," J retorts "rapist."

The weekly Wednesday morning market is the center of conviviality without frustration. One meets everyone including "foreign" friends from the surrounding villages. Our town has always been the market center for the three or four smaller villages around it.

Aside from fruits, vegetables, two fish stalls, and a butcher, there is a panoply of stands selling incredibly cheap clothes, jewelry and bags (all made in China) and colorful Provençal tablecloths. My greatest buy was a black tufted short jacket for five euros, great for doggie walking but equally respectable for any occasion. On a Wednesday, a few weeks after I bought it, the vendor came over to me. "Didn't I see you at the market in Aix?" she asked. "I told my husband how chic you looked wearing our jacket. But of course, you had a Louis Vuitton bag with you." Frenchwomen of all classes are up on their status symbols. Dear reader, please note the bag was a present from my kids to mark my coming of age. Don't ask which.

The absolute king of the market is the chicken man. The smell of slowly spit-roasting chicken wafts over the market. It is irresistible. Everyone, including me, lines up patiently for his chicken to be pulled off the spit. The first time I came to acquire this delicacy, *Monsieur Poulet* looked at me with the arrogance of a snooty *maitre d'hotel*. *"Avez-vous réservé,"* he demanded.

Reserved! I wasn't planning lunch at Maxim's. I just wanted to buy a chicken (*Poulet* in French). "This time, I will make an exception and give you one but, *Madame*, it is imperative that you reserve your chicken in advance." Which, believe me I now do!

Monseiur Poulet, well rounded and rosy cheeked, keeps up a running dialogue with his customers, asking about their health, their love life, their kids, as well as expounding his thoughts on the weather, politics, national and local, and especially on the terrible state of the French economy. Knowing I am a foreigner, he asks me to corroborate his opinions. He seems to think this gives them more weight. I always agree with him.

Finally, my chicken is nestled into its bag accompanied by a huge scoop of potatoes, which have been browned underneath the dripping chicken fat. I try to refuse this delicacy causing *Monseiur* to regard me with total amazement. "You don't like my potatoes! How can you even think of eating the chicken without them? They are my special combination." It would really be useless to try to explain about low-fat diets. When I go to retrieve J reading his paper and sipping a pastis, the first thing he asks is "Did you get the chicken?"

At lunch I try to get J to take off the crispy skin and only eat a few potatoes. But this is extremely unproductive. He eats every bit of the chicken and almost all the potatoes, looking at me with total joy. I feed him boiled fish and vegetables the next day to satisfy his cholesterol.

The flower man is my friend. He always gives me a few roses free. However, I am a client only in winter. When I explained that, in summer, I have lots of flowers in the garden, which I cut for bouquets, he looked at me dolefully. "When you cut flowers, you make the stars cry." I assume his flowers arrive from heaven, packed in bunches and ready for sale, without the benefit of clippers.

The mayor uses the market for networking. He smiles and shakes a lot of hands, trying to win over the socialists. I made his acquaintance when he picked me up off the street after I was run over by a fat lady driving a mean shopping cart. Since then he greets me with a nod of his head and very, very slight bow. No handshake though. I guess he knows I'm not entitled to vote.

Three times a week, Monday, Wednesday and Friday, we have our own little social gathering at home. This is the ritual cup of coffee with Marie, our gym teacher, or more fashionably, "personal trainer," after an hour of grueling exercises. The conversation varies from politics, music, gardening, shopping and, of course, hair styles, face lifts and our husbands" faults. When it gets to this low level, J leaves to do more important things

Marie came to us through our source of almost everything – Victor. She lives in the next village and arrives in the morning at exactly 9 o'clock, not a minute before, not a minute after. Petite with the strength of a six-foot truck driver, she can do amazing things with her body. That she expects the same from us is a tribute to her unbounded optimism. The dogs adore her, and they also attend classes. They settle into their favorite positions as soon as we start the warm up. Alias is banished *au lit* (to her bed) during the horizontal part of the session since she also lies down – with her head on my chest. She is now so well-trained she disappears as soon as we hit the floor. Marie is not a believer in mechanical contrivances and considers the mental concentration as important as the physical. J has a problem with this and often drifts off into another world, brought back to reality by a sharp *"Tenez vos abdos."* (Hold your stomach in). I concentrate so hard on mine that sometimes I feel like a spoon, hollow side up. Marie approves.

Although we do not work out on machines, she brings with her lots of other instruments of torture. There are bright colored elastics, which used in the right way, can make you feel you will never be able to sit again. There are weights, which normally we can cope with except when we are forced to stand on a wobbly rubber disc making it very hard to keep your balance unless, indeed, you get your stomach so tight it presses against your vertebrae. There are also things to squeeze between your thighs and a weight on your head, so you don't slouch. But even the most classic exercises like push-ups, sit-ups, getting your head to practically touch the floor without bending a knee are subject to very strict control by Marie. She notices and corrects every infraction. If your legs are in the air, your tailbone still has to be on the ground. One leg up, one leg down for sixteen times requires breathing through your chest. *Abdos* are nailed to the ground and not to be released.

Marie works a lot on our equilibrium believing this is very important as one grows "older." J is very proud since he can stand on one leg like a heron for much longer than I can. She also teaches us how to bend down to pick something up like a tenor dropping on one knee during an aria and not like your old grandfather. Obviously, we also must practice arising gracefully without falling on our faces.

Besides our quaint village life, we do have more sophisticated events on our social calendar. I have always loved music although I can neither play an instrument, read notes or manage to sing "Happy Birthday" on key. In Amsterdam, we had a yearly subscription to the opera at the *Musiek theater* (Music Theater) and the Concertgebouw (concert hall).

When we came to live here permanently, one of the first things we did was attempt to get a subscription to the Marseille opera, which is renowned not only for great quality but for discovering new talent. This is the Provençal equivalent of trying to get a season ticket for the Met or La Scala. The Marseillaise love their opera and subscriptions are passed down from father to son. Normally you have to wait until someone dies. J doesn't have that much patience so by pulling lots of strings and a great deal of persistence he succeeded in procuring our tickets, an aisle seats at that. J gets claustrophobic sitting in the middle of the row in case he should have to get up to pee. This has never happened.

We opted for Sunday matinee for the practical reason that driving home at midnight from Marseille, especially in winter, didn't seem too attractive. Our more savvy friends were horrified. "Don't you know that Sunday matinee is the crutch and cane crowd?" Since we didn't get the connotation right away, one explained, "You know – old. You should have taken the premiere soirée. That's when everyone goes." Considering that there is never an empty seat on Sunday, there are some others besides "everyone." Anyway, it makes us feel young!

There is a ritual attached to Sunday at the opera. We always have lunch in the same restaurant with the other old (literally and figuratively) opera goers. The restaurant is Italian and hardly chic, set on a street with rather questionable cafés, but walking distance to the opera. *Madame*, the proprietor, is small, plump and Marseillaise from the top of her well-coiffed head to her pointed shoes. Because so many of the opera personnel, including often the singers, eat here, she is always invited to the dress rehearsals. Before we have even looked at the menu, we get a professional opinion on the production we are about to see. "Ah, the tenor, supreme, *magnifique.* But the soprano. A real screecher. The décor is minable (miserable). They obviously did it on a shoestring. The costumes weren't too bad though except that awful soprano looked like a sausage. Pay attention to the conductor. Never have I heard such a wonderful sound."

We always order the same thing. Tiny fried octopus to begin and then a spicy lasagna and an open carafe of red wine. "Don't bother with a bottle," *Madame* advises, "the open wine is just as good. I buy it to drink with what I cook. "I think she is secretly in love with J. Several times during the meal, she passes by and plants a kiss on top of his (bald) head. I get a smooch on the way out.

The day ends with practically the whole of the audience waiting in line to feed either money or a credit card to one of the two machines at the parking garage. The credit card machine takes longer to verify 4 euros than a purchase of 400 anywhere else. One time the machine devoured J's card, causing great panic. A mechanic had to be called to retrieve it. I must say the long cue behind was very patient, although some switched machines and became cash customers. Since then, we too prefer to pay in real money.

In summer, Provence sings, swings and makes music of every sort. It all begins on June 21st the longest day of the year and the official beginning of summer with "*La Nuit de la Musique*" (the night of music). From Paris to the smallest village, the streets ring with the sound of music. From professional jazz groups to a lonely harpist, every musician worth his salt participates in this tribute to the power of music. From hard rock to samba to Mozart, this open-air concert offers a variety of unimaginable sounds, some haunting and magnificent, others requiring ear plugs.

Although our village is also an enthusiastic participant in this ode to music, we have the tradition of going to Aix-en-Provence, sitting at a café on the Cours Mirabeau, and listening to the greatest and most varied groups of wandering minstrels for the price of a pastis accompanied by free olives. Our friend Roby who plays a mean saxophone takes to the street with a couple of other "senior" jazz musicians. We offer them a beer as they pass by.

More serious is the Aix-en-Provence Festival. It used to be only opera and mostly Mozart but in recent years it has expanded to include concerts, chamber music and recitals by young musicians. Although there is a real effort to make performances more accessible to ordinary mortals as well as children, it still remains a rather pricey and snobby event. It does, however, give me a chance to wear something besides jeans.

The Aixoise are very conservative and balk at a contemporary décor of Don Giovanni or anything else that challenges their concept of what opera should be. Still the festival is one of the highlights of our summer life. We bite the bullet and take tickets for lots of things. Since it costs so much, J no longer sleeps through the first act of the opera, but he still has a tendency to drift off occasionally during a symphony since there is not much visual excitement.

Some of the operas are given in the courtyard of the Archbishop's Palace. There has not been an archbishop in residence for ages, but I like to think they are listening from above, (or perhaps below!) It is a theatre under the stars, not too large but with perfect acoustics. Since summer nights can be cold in Provence, the management lays blankets on every few seats for those optimists who came in sleeveless dresses.

At a performance of "The Marriage of Figaro," J and I did not have seats together, having booked at the last minute. I was delighted to find a blanket on mine. By the second act, it started to get chilly and I threw the blanket elegantly around my shoulders. The man next to me dressed in a short-sleeved polo shirt was starting to turn blue.

"*Monsieur,*" I asked, "would you like to share my blanket." I used the word couverture which is more a bed cover instead of "plaid" which means a small throw, (nothing to do with Scottish clans) so he looked a bit shocked but since he was basically freezing to death, he nodded with a "*Oui, merci.*"

Huddled under one blanket with a perfect stranger does make for some verbal contact. At the intermission, he told me his wife was sitting somewhere else as well, and then proceeded to enlighten me on the finer points of the production and Mozart's message in this opera. He was not enthusiastic about the stage setting. "Mozart would be horrified," he declared. We were still engrossed in conversation under the blanket, when J and my companion's wife came by, almost simultaneously.

My blanket partner sheepishly followed his wife. I could hear him explaining how this nice American lady had kept him warm. J looked at me rather oddly. "Why were you under a blanket with that guy?"

"He was cold," I replied.

"Cold"! exclaimed J. "I wasn't cold at all."

He had taken the precautionary measures of wearing a heavy sweater, jacket and a chic cashmere scarf around his neck. Nevertheless, after the intermission, I again offered half the cover to my friend, which he took with a grateful smile. At the end of the performance, he whispered *"Merci pour une soirée si sympathique,"* (Thanks for a lovely evening) and disappeared into the crowd.

The oldest festival in France dating from 1869 is in Orange. Called *Chorégies de Orange*, it is held every July and August in the most complete, best preserved Roman amphitheater in the world. The stage is about 130 feet tall, originally decorated with columns, some of which, recently unearthed, have been placed back in their original positions. About 80 feet up, an imposing statue of a Roman emperor surveys the crowds before him, which in the old days might have reached around 8000 spectators. He has a removable head. In Roman times, when the emperor changed, so did the head. I wonder what they did with all the old heads. Needless to say, with all this original décor, complicated stage settings are not absolutely necessary.

To see "La Boheme" or hear Mozart's requiem in this magnificent ancient theatre with stars shining overhead and a sliver of moon is a magic experience. You forget the discomfort. And believe me it is not a comfortable seat at the Met. Stone ledges carved into a hill on which the derrieres of many Romans rested – I am sure without complaint but perhaps they were better padded than me – can be less than pleasurable. But this obstacle is easily overcome. You take cushions with you. The night of a performance in Orange, 5000 people walk around carrying pillows.

We always eat in the same restaurant just across from the amphitheater. During the rest of the year, it is a small place with a terrace in summer. Nothing extraordinary. But on the evenings of a festival performance, it is transformed into a super-chic mess hall. One menu, no choice (except the wine since no self-respecting Frenchman would accept someone else dictating what he drinks.), one price. At least 100 opera fans crowd onto the terrace. How they manage to get everyone served and out in time for the performance is a Herculean feat. Resounding warning music starts emanating from loudspeakers around the theatre about three quarters of an hour before the start, making me extremely nervous. Experience has shown there is plenty of time to linger over a coffee, or to wait in line for the one co-ed toilet Only those ascending into the alpine realms need to leave early. It's a long climb. When I order tickets, I explain very clearly that I have a fear of heights so strong that I might just jump from on high onto the stage. Until now, I have always managed not to sit above the tenth row.

The magic spell is sometimes broken by the mistral sweeping through the theatre at what seems like 100 miles an hour. It can blow the cape off the tenor and totally destroy the soprano's coiffure, not to mention what it does to the acoustics. When this wind is predicted, it is advisable to arrive in a fur coat or at least a down jacket. They don't give out 5,000 blankets! Rain, which is rarer, can also spoil the evening. If it occurs after the first act, your money is not returned. People are inclined to wait out the storm and don't seem to mind watching the second act, drenched to the skin.

There are many, many music festivals all over Provence. Our village has a 3-day jazz marathon in the courtyard of the local château. Accompanied by free wine and pizza at one euro a slice, this is an event not to be missed. All the winegrowers in the region use the opportunity to promote their wine and the rest of us profit from the effort.

In the tiny village of La Coste in the Vaucluse, the marquis de Sade's old castle has been taken over by Pierre Cardin and turned into a chic site for music and theater catering to the swishy Parisian set who have vacation homes nearby in the Luberon. Confronted with this snobbish, couture-clad crowd, I feel like I arrived from the provinces, which I did. No communal blankets here – just cashmere shawls. J comes in jeans and sweater and feels totally comfortable.

There is a world- renowned piano festival at Le Roc d'Antheron on the grounds of the château. Twenty years ago, one sat on the grass under huge plane trees and listened to the world's top pianists play on a stage in the middle of a small artificial lake. Although the stage still floats, much else has changed. Bleachers have been erected, prices have gone up and tickets hard to come by. Nevertheless, the charm persists. You can still picnic on the grounds either with your own food or more comfortably in an open-air restaurant. Champagne and wine flow freely. It's a Provençal Glynebourne.

Since 2007, the end of summer no longer heralds a cultural winter hibernation. Le Grand Theatre de Provence has opened its doors in Aix-en-Provence. The decision to build it within walking distance of the Cours Mirabeau, which is the center of the city, was a wonderful choice. Unfortunately, the building itself is a tribute to horrendous architecture. Covered with some awful, expensive stone, it is built on several levels with 6,000 square meters of huge open terraces, which serve no discernable purpose and are only reached by climbing hundreds of steps. For the breathless, there is an elevator somewhere inside the theatre. Frank Lloyd Wright would roll over in his grave and Frank Gehry would roll his eyes. The Italian architect who designed it is certainly no match for his ancestors who constructed the amphitheater in Orange. Inside the decoration is slightly better but there are many no- view or partial- view seats and an appalling lack of adequate toilet facilities. Not exactly one's idea of a theater for the 21st century.

But, the program of events more than makes up for the architectural disaster. Dance, opera recitals, chamber music, jazz, orchestras, violinists, trios, quartets, and even musicals including a production of "Fame" in French. We have a subscription to ten different performances. These soirées entail getting dressed up, meeting friends for a before theatre dinner, champagne at the intermission and a glass of wine after the performance. We feel like we live in New York. The drive back to the country doesn't take much longer than a cab from the theatre district to the Upper West-Side.

More of New York in Aix. We go to the Met once a month, via the direct telecasting of their best operas in HD. We enter our very comfortable seats in the Cézanne cinema at about the same time our co-viewers take theirs in Lincoln Center. But we are better placed and pay a fraction of what they do. We also have the advantage of being up close – sometimes a bit too much so – right into the nose hairs of the tenor. Another plus point, we are allowed to go back stage and watch all the scenery being moved around and listen to interviews with the stars. Between acts, we, too, get to drink a glass of champagne thanks to the restaurant next door that sets up their table during intermission. No one goes into the cinema lobby for popcorn and a coke. This is a pure opera experience.

Country bumpkins we may be a good part of the time, but we are not culture deprived. If variety is the spice of life, we live a hot curry.

CHAPTER 5

THE ANIMAL KINGDOM

Today I found a dead mouse on the kitchen floor and believe it or not I rejoiced! Better than all the live ones making ca-ca on my kitchen counter. But brave I am not, so Claudie, my *gardien's* wife, picked it up by the tail with a scissors, effectively cutting the tail in half. Gross! I offered her a plastic bag as a saner solution.

I have a thing about mice – especially since they ate all the wires connecting the dishwasher, without getting electrocuted, and built a nest with dog croquettes in the motor. 200 Euros and two weeks of eight people in the house very unaccustomed to hand washing dishes was the price we paid. "Close the door to the kitchen" was the repairman's advice with a big Provençal ha-ha laugh. My friend was luckier. She found a mouse in the machine and just turned on the hot cycle.

There seems to be an attraction in electrical wires. Ants devoured the wires of our neighbor's automatic gate. They couldn't get in or out for days. Fortunately, our ants are into breadcrumbs but then again, we have a gate that hands open.

Among other unwanted visitors are bunny rabbits. Cute, adorable bunnies with big ears and cotton ball tails – not one or two but seemingly hundreds. I understand now the saying about having kids like rabbits. They wreak havoc everywhere. Any new plant did not survive the first night. Leaves were chewed up, rosebuds devoured, young tomato plants stripped bare, lower branches of expensive and well-cared for bushes were gnawed. They dug holes big enough for a grave, tunneled their way through the protective fence around the vegetable garden, pushed away, evidently with the strength of Atlas, rocks placed blocking their underground passages.

Remembering the book "Watershed Down," told from a rabbit's point of view, where the human meanies flooded their warrens with water, I suggested to the *gardien* that he should put the hose in the holes. Apparently, our rabbits can swim and just dug their way out at the other end. Our three dogs spend their days chasing rabbits, without great results. Occasionally, the smallest dog, Txonny, dines on rabbit innards and we find a tail, some paws or ears on the terrace. Alias, our sometimes hunter, managed to nab one which she placed on the white couch, sitting proudly beside it.

Desperation calls for Herculean measures. My son suggested we put a sign up – "Free Carrots Next Door." Claudie thought it was more practical just to strew carrots on the terrace in case the rabbits were illiterate. But apparently, carrots are for domesticated rabbits without opportunities to munch in nature.

Only one of the dogs took a bite out of a carrot. The bunnies continued on their rampage.

Our electrician, Pierre, had an eco-friendly solution, albeit not bunny friendly. He would come with a ferret. A ferret absolutely loves to drink rabbit blood. He would put the vampire ferret in the rabbit hole and Count Dracula would bite one or two bunnies in the neck and feast on their blood. Meanwhile the other rabbits anxious to avoid the same fate would flee the warren and be caught in the net placed by Pierre. This gory solution did not result in the massacre I had hoped for. Total catch, 2 rabbits – dinner for 4 maybe. I wondered though why an electrician has a killer ferret. I soon found out.

Pierre assembled his troops, hunters from the *Federation de la Chasse* (Association of the Hunt). They arrived eight strong equipped with various cages and six ferrets. The operation was humanitarian rabbit control. The ferrets would be placed in the rabbit warrens, scaring them (unfortunately not to death) and they would flee into the waiting cages. The hunters, instead of feasting on their booty, would load the cages into their various vehicles and free the rabbits in a specially designated reservation for displaced bunnies. When they are acclimated, they are then let loose into nature. I have the feeling they all found their way back to their country club *chez nous.*

The hunters happily reported a total haul of 18 alive. One met its death in the teeth of a ferret.

Refusing any sort of monetary reward, they graciously accepted a liquid one. We sat around the pool as they related their various hunting adventures from wild boar to birds. Glass after glass was filled and emptied. The fattest and the jolliest of the group clasped his ferret tenderly in his arms the whole time. He generously invited me to hold the ferret for a while. I looked at the beast, he at me and we both decided we were not for each other. I bravely, however, patted its ugly head, keeping well away from the murderous teeth.

Still the plague continued. Eighteen rabbits did not decimate the population. I also discovered our rabbits lived in an apartheid environment. The ordinary brown ones lived on the right side of the vineyards and *les lapins rousses,* (reddish rabbits), appropriately enough, on the left side.

Finally, our *gardien*, Robert, decided. *"Assez!"* (enough is enough). The only way to get rid of the rabbit plague, he informed me, was to shoot them, at least some of them which might give the message to the rest. This solution posed a few problems, none of them however unsolvable. First of all, it would have to be done very secretively since it was not the hunting season. Secondly, Robert had no gun and you can't even buy bullets here without a license and then only in season. Victor, our tennis pro offered to buy (or obtain by other means) bullets on his next trip to Italy. The Italians, seemingly are not squeamish about trafficking bullets any time of the year. Robert would borrow a shotgun from his father and "voila" end of the rabbit terror.

So, with the arrival of the bullets and the weapon, Robert set out late each night and bagged a few. Don't ask me what he did with them. I don't want to know. The French are very fond of *lapin à la moutarde* (rabbit in mustard sauce). Evidently, the message did get through loud and clear. I still see long ears scurrying here and there and an occasionally nibbled-on plant or a new hole, but more or less damage control has been affected. In my city-oriented heart, I really find it hard killing any living creature except really vile things like rats and destructive mice or cockroaches, but I am now a country dweller, and this seems to be the way it goes here.

Unknowingly rubbing salt in the wound, an artist friend in China sent me a Christmas card wishing me "a great Year of the Rabbit." Three beautifully drawn bunnies decorated this poisoned wish.

Other unwanted but much more dangerous visitors are *frelons* (hornets!) Locals warn -and I don't question it – two love stings and you're a goner. Every August, they install themselves in the tree shading our summer outdoor couches. They can't seem to learn this is not a safe place for us or them. Our plan of action involves calling the *pompiers* (firemen) who arrive at night – when all the hornets are at home and hopefully asleep – dressed in white from head to toe with a hood and mask protecting their faces. Reminds me most of Neil Armstrong landing on the moon.

It is extremely impressive to watch, and one of the highlights of our grandchildren's visits. I tremble in terror that someone will be stung but this has never happened. The fireman is posed on a huge ladder, steadied and watched by two colleagues, since the plane tree the hornets occupy is over 20 meters tall. He sprays some powerful poison which works very well and then he removes the nest. The phrase "hornet's nest" has taken on a new meaning. This service used to be free with remuneration at the discretion of the client. It is now a paying business for which we happily dig deep into our pockets. The hornet extermination session usually ends with ice cold cokes and some snacks for the heroes.

Fireman play a very important role in life in France. Not only in fighting bravely the many forest fires which occur almost every summer when the mistral, the violent wind from the north blows, these raging blazes usually occur through someone's carelessness – a burning cigarette thrown from a car window, an untended barbecue or often deliberately set by a pyromaniac

But firemen in France are also the ones you call for any emergency – indeed for hornets – but also for a heart attack victim. They are the first to give aid at an accident and are credited with saving many, many lives. It somehow gives one a very secure feeling, living in a small village and knowing that professional, and kind, help is only a phone call away.

You can call them as well when the displaced population of a bees' nest decide to cuddle next to your pool, which has happened to us twice. But not to kill them. Bees are a protected species by law and the firemen will put you in touch with a bona fide *apiculteur* (beekeeper). Our friendly *pompiers* decide who is the best one and call for us, and then we wait for the professional bee savior to arrive.

The first episode brought us a young man, wearing shorts, a pony tail and not much else, not even shoes. Equipped with a box and a spray can filled with a mixture of sweet smelling herbs, he first sat down to talk to his clients. Whispering sweet nothings in their ears, he was rewarded by the bees crawling all over him. Slowly he started spraying, and like sheep the bees began entering the box in very orderly fashion. "I'll be back again after dark," he informed us, to get the ones who are out for the day. They always come back at dark." They did and so did he. Over a cool glass of rosé, he explained he had loved bees all his life. "They are fascinating," he recounted," their social structure, their work ethics, the class division."

When asked if he could really make a good living out of just keeping bees, in true flowerchild philosophy, he replied "That is not the essence of my life."

Our second bee keeper the next year – I think there's something about us that attracts lost bees – was quite another type, although in his way also quite spiritual. Is this perhaps a necessary quality in dealing with bees? At least 40 years the senior of our last hippy bee collector, he had the air of a true country gentleman. Dressed in corduroy knickerbockers, leather vest and plaid shirt, a scarf casually knotted around his neck with a well-trimmed grey beard and a full head of hair, he was most attractive. He apologized for keeping us waiting but he had to get his equipment together. The major equipment consisted of a box, the herbal mixture to be sprayed and a brush and dustpan. When he saw the sorry state of the bees huddled together in a mass on the gravel, he was visibly saddened. "Ah, all the rain and wind has weakened them. Probably no queen either." Putting a tiny bit of honey inside the box, he started spraying and, more or less, shoveling the poor things in.

Naturally, I invited him into the kitchen for the usual glass of rosé. I was also very curious to find out how he became a keeper of bees. "Well, he told me, my father kept bees as a hobby and as a child, I always loved them. But my father was a rich man and didn't need to work. He could spend all his time doing exactly what he wanted, including dispersing the entire family fortune. My life was stress, stress, stress, trying to earn more and more money until, finally, I was lucky enough to have a heart attack which didn't kill me but changed my life. I decided to keep bees which had been my dream for 40 years."

At that moment, my husband who had missed all the bee excitement, being locked up in front of his computer as usual, descended the stairs into the kitchen. He stopped dead in his tracks with such a look of astonishment, you would have thought he had caught me *en flagrante* instead of having a glass of wine at the kitchen table with, albeit, a very

103

handsome man. "I'll be back tomorrow night" announced the beekeeper, "to get the rest."

"Who on earth was that?" Asked J. When I explained, all I got was "harrumph." Could it be the sting of jealousy? Great afternoon for me!

Other small creatures that live with us rent-free are goldfish and frogs. The frogs hang out around our large basin as well as in the small one and they communicate loud and strong. Their love songs in spring may seem sexy and melodious to frog ears but it drives us crazy. Croak, croak, croak through half the day and all night. Compared to this cacophony, atonal modern music sounds like Mozart. They also literally croak (die) for love. It seems they battle to death for the favors of a female. I found one lifeless frog floating around in the water and another at the end of the vegetable garden. I didn't try kissing them to see if my prince would arrive. I screamed for J.

The fish, however, are extremely quiet residents. At the sound of my footsteps crunching on the gravel, they swim to the side for a meal. One has a very distinct personality. It is a huge carp that has been swimming around for at least twenty years. When I come to the edge of the water, calling "Fish, come," he does. I can pat him, he sucks my finger, and eats out of my hand. (No, this is not a fishy story).

Counted among the serious invaders of our domain, are *sangliers,* (wild boars), except that they are not so wild having been crossed years ago with pigs. We live in the middle of hunting country and la chasse is the major distraction from October to April for macho men who still feel the need to bring home the beast. Killing animals, although I am aware of all the reasons why this is necessary to keep the animal population in control, really is not very appealing to me. Each Sunday when hunters and their dogs corner the wild boars for a good shoot, I can hear the yelps of the dogs, but also the screaming of the *sangliers.* Needless to say, I was rooting for the boars until they started to party at our tennis in the summer. "I know where the boars do it," my 13-year-old granddaughter announced.

And did they do it! Grass dug up, huge holes, plants trampled on. They even came as far as the swimming pool. I suppose they got high on chlorinated water. The need for action was apparent and we tried all sorts of solutions –anti-*sanglier* stinky poles, loud music at night to discourage them from coming too close (if you ask me, they just boogied to it), a hidden hunter waiting all night to shoot one. Totally illegal out of season.

Nothing but nothing discouraged them to give up their country club membership and we finally resorted to a low electrified wire fence around our huge rambling property. I suppose one or two got a shock, seeing there were paw prints under the wire and the others took the hint. The wild boar problem was solved at the cost of a first-class trip around the world! On a cynical note: They moved over to our neighbors who were obliged to wire their property too.

I guess things with wings like birds and chickens are part of the animal realm.

I'm not particularly fond of flying objects like birds and bats. Bats flying through open windows in the summer are a perpetual nightmare. All the women in the house run screaming into the garden, terrified of a bat becoming entangled in their long curly locks. I know this is a myth and try to reassure my guests, but I have a hard time myself with panic control. Other encounters with bats which really freak me out are when I open a long-closed shuttered window somewhere on the top floor to find a string of them hanging upside down. Then I do scream for help.

Birds are also on my list of things I hate, in contrast to the rest of the world. Bird watching, bird calls, bird baths are all things that I cannot even imagine. When a group of sparrows sweep down to drink out of our pool, I stand up and screech like a banshee to scare them away.

Nevertheless, birds seem to be very attracted to our trees. For years, we had a very discreet couple (blackbirds) who arrived every spring to build their nest in one of the plane trees – of course the one shading our table. Every visit to the tree is well documented.

This year they brought some friends. Now we have three couples constructing nests. You cannot imagine what they use. Materials they don't manage to get into the nests are strewn around the tree. We find pieces of cord used to tie up vines, all sizes of branches, straw and occasionally some cotton wool. I have no idea where that comes from. Aside from making a mess, they are noisy. Real tweeting gossips.

Some birds prefer a more sheltered environment. I found a cute little nest on the window sill of one of our not often used bathrooms, with six very tiny eggs in it. I controlled the urge to throw the thing down two stories to the ground below. Instead, I found myself peeking through the window every day and watching mama bird sitting quietly on her eggs. If she even caught a glimpse of me, she flew off. And then it happened. There were six tiny, tiny babies, huddled together, beaks wide open, awaiting dinner. But, as is the way of the world, one morning all that was left were six empty eggs. I know now where the phrase empty nest syndrome comes from.

I have also decided to include chickens, albeit not mine, in the animal world. This thanks to my friend Denise, who has had some very emotional fowl experiences. She has five adopted chickens, Martha, Mabel, Mildred, Marilyn and Millicent who follow her like pets and produce dozens of eggs, which she occasionally gives me as a gift. I totally ignore J's cholesterol on such occasions and make a six egg omelet.

Chickens sometimes need rather wondrous treatments to cure various health problems. When Mabel was not her usual clucking self, just moping around instead of producing eggs, Denise phoned a friendly fowl specialist. "She probably has an egg stuck," replied the professional. "This is what you do. Boil a pot of water and hold the chicken's bottom over it until the egg pops out." One way to make a really fresh soft-boiled egg.

Capturing Mabel was not so easy, she being a shy chick. Finally, Denise managed to scoop her up, tucked her under her elbow, derriere facing forward and held the right part over the steaming pot, massaging gently. *Et voila!* Out came a very crushed egg. Mabel sighed with relief and in Denise's own words, "now produces *obies* (torpedoes)." For further advice on the perils of keeping chickens, Denise just Googles "sick chick."

Unfortunately, disaster struck one day at dusk.

In summer the chickens have the run of the place, "free-range," as it is proudly labeled on supermarket fowl. One balmy evening Denise came home from work to find a trail of blood, feathers, a few loose legs and only Mabel sitting contentedly in the coop. The four others had been spirited away, probably by a fox having a dinner party. Denise was distraught but the brave pioneer woman that she is, she went out the next day and bought four others. Now into the N's of chicken naming there was Nina, Nellie, Nora and in a lack of inspiration but alphabetically correct, No Name.

The empty nest was replenished – but not for long! A few weeks later, Nina was the victim. One of the neighbors suggested maybe it wasn't a fox but another neighbor's big black dog. (Neighborly relations are a whole other chapter.) Nina was gone but poor Nora had been attacked and to Denise's horror was totally paralyzed. Nora, wrapped in Denise's cashmere shawl, was packed off to the vet with great speed. "Well," said the vet, "she might just recover spontaneously. Keep her warm and wait until tomorrow." To his credit, and my amazement, he didn't blink an eyelash at what is normally regarded in this part of France as food, as a paid patient.

But it wasn't to be. The next morning Nora was just as immobile. Again, to the vet where she was mercifully sent to the big chicken coop in the sky — at a cost of 80 Euros! A mutual friend was horrified. "Couldn't you have just wrung her neck?" Denise's eyes filled with tears at such a cruel remark. Well it's how most chickens get to meet their maker!

But there is a more to merciful way to put a chicken to death. Another friend offered Denise her method. "I just put it in the car, turn on the motor, close the windows and the garage door and *voila.*"

Like people there are also four- footed visitors who drop in uninvited. Our favorites are a porcupine who delighted our grandchildren and a small fox who came to dinner a couple of times. A very disgusting toad appeared now and then and peed on our front steps.

CHAPTER 6

A DOG'S LIFE IN PROVENCE

Undoubtedly the kings or I should say one king and two queens of our animal kingdom are the three very spoiled, demanding, undisciplined dogs whom we love to death. None of the three came as puppies and two were not even chosen by us. As coincidence would have it, our daughter and her husband moved from a large house at the sea to an apartment in Barcelona at the same time we came to live permanently in Provence. They had the most beautiful long-haired German shepherd I have ever seen, Gypsy, who was a treasured summer visitor along with my daughter and family. The dog put terror into the heart of most of our guests, workmen, the mail lady and anyone else who happened to wander on to our property by her appearance, but I have never known such a gentle, well-tempered dog.

She was the guardian of all our grandchildren. They could dress her up, pull her tail, sit on her, hug and kiss her and she accepted it all. She followed them everywhere, springing into the pool and swimming next to them to make sure they were not in danger. But she was not an apartment dog. "Mom" said my daughter in one of her infrequent telephone calls, "I have really good news for you. You know how much you love Gypsy. Well now she can come to live with you full time because she really wouldn't be happy in the city;"

Without a moment of doubt, I replied "That's wonderful. You can see her whenever you visit."

"Oh, just one more thing. You have to take Txonny as well."

"Who or what on earth is Txonny?"

"Txonny is adorable," answered my daughter coolly. "Gypsy saved her life and now they are inseparable, so you see there's no other way."

"Of course, darling, I love the idea of having two dogs."

"Good then it's settled. You can pick them up this weekend. Bye."

Maybe she just forgot Barcelona is not around the corner but over 500 kilometers away. Just what I need, a canine I have never seen, but anything for Gypsy and my daughter. Txonny turned out to be a rather ugly hairy mutt, but as my daughter had said, sweet and loving, and so our life changed to accommodate two dogs. Until a year later.

"What!" I heard J shout through the phone. "Absolutely not! No! I'll pass your mother."

"I have really good news for you" said my daughter. As soon as I hear this I know an enormous favor is going to be asked of me. "We have bought you the rattan chairs and table you wanted for the

113

terrace and they will be delivered tomorrow. Oh, and I am also sending Pinxo. He doesn't like city life." Pinxo had been acquired to fill the empty nest when Gypsy left, his size being more suited to apartment living. I had made his barking acquaintance in Barcelona and was not impressed. Although J kind of liked walking around the city with Pinxo on a leash. He did attract a lot of attention, this tall bearded man with a small white dog. I remember coming out of Cartier (just buying pen refills) and seeing J surrounded by admiring females, canine and human.

The van arrived with our terrace furniture and a small cage containing a white, yapping monster demanding to be let out IMMEDIATELY. He took one look around, sniffed at the two females, thought he had landed in paradise, and declared himself "master of the universe." Txonny was very impressed. Gypsy regarded him as nothing more than a small nuisance. He was more than a nuisance – he was a real pain in the neck. However, under the stern glare of Gypsy who quickly taught him some manners like not eating out of her bowl, not mounting either her or Txonny, and not installing himself anywhere near her, he somewhat settled down and life became a little more bearable.

Since arriving, Pinxo had never left my side, following me like a stalker, so when he disappeared one fine day, panic broke out. J and I, the guardien and his wife spread out in four directions, calling "Pinxo, Pinxo, come here, *viens ici*." I was in tears. It's amazing how one becomes attached to even a pesky, terribly behaved, second-hand dog. Just as acute despair was about to set in, our neighbor Frederic, the manager of the wine chateau next door, came to the door carrying a very subdued Pinxo.

"Where did you find him," asked J.

Looking a little bit uncomfortable and kind of moving from one foot to the other, Frederic recounted: "I was just about to leave for lunch when Gypsy came up the stairs into the office and started tugging at my sleeve. I know that sometimes she guards the office, making sure no clients can enter, but this was different. I followed her outside to my truck, the dog barking all the time, running in front, so what could I do. I just drove behind her up the mountain road for about a kilometer or two and there was Pinxo. So that's how I found him. Gypsy led me to him." He cleared his throat and explained, "I guess this sounds like a kind of bizarre story but really, it's true."

Bizarre or not, we immediately gave him the customary reward – a glass of his own rosé. Pinxo, his usual annoying traits restored, barked at him the whole time. NB: This is not a shaggy dog story!

But in all fairness, Gypsy was not a totally angelic dog. Although she did not beg at the table or steal food, she would hang under the kids" chairs hoping one would drop something, which was inevitable. So, we trusted her completely – until one night. I had invited some friends, as well as the new neighbors who had just taken over the vineyards.

As it happened my best friend from New York was also here. I decided to do a really classic French meal, *gigot* (leg of lamb), *pomme de terre au gratin*, (potatoes topped with cheese and cream), lima beans and fresh string beans. The leg of lamb beautifully prepared, salted and peppered, stuck with fresh garlic cloves and with branches of rosemary surrounding it in the earthenware casserole, was put on the kitchen counter to rest while I went to get dressed.

Descending the stairs about a half hour later, hopefully as Frenchly chic as my dinner, I perceived something strange lying in the middle of the hall carpet. Upon closer scrutiny, I realized what it was. A totally bare bone which had once held my beautiful roast.

"Yikes!" I screamed and raced to the kitchen. Sure enough, there was the casserole in several pieces on the kitchen floor bare of all contents. Gypsy was splayed out in the TV room in a lamb-induced drug state. She had eaten it all, the meat, the garlic, even the rosemary.

With fifteen minutes until our guests' arrival, obviously some really creative thinking was needed. Ever resourceful, Roz coolly announced, "We'll make the pastrami." A New Yorker, she never arrived in France without a supply of the Big Apple's goodies – bagels, lox, kosher dill pickles, vitamins – and pastrami.

"What!" I answered. "Pastrami with potato gratin? And besides it isn't cooked."

"We'll microwave it," and with that proceeded to squeeze the pastrami into a dish which would fit into the microwave.

"How long," I worried.

"No idea, we'll play it by ear." I found this a rather odd term for the preparation of my fancy dinner but then again what choice did I have."

The dinner was a huge success. The first course being *foie gras,* accompanied by a *confit* of onion and a Beaume de Venise, was well appreciated. If anyone found the pastrami (splendidly cooked by ear) with its accompaniments an odd combination, they kept it to themselves. Personally, I prefer my pastrami with potato salad and coleslaw. The wine, a magnificent Bordeaux carefully chosen for the gigot, and now accompanying pastrami, was downed by everyone with gusto and many compliments. In all the years in France I have learned one important lesson. Good wine makes up for anything. Gypsy was persona non-grata in the house for two days because of massive farting attacks.

In the way of the world, Gypsy grew old and finally exchanged the here and now for the hereafter. We were devastated. The guardian walked around the property for two days crying and me too. Our grandchildren swore they would remember her forever. The house seemed rather odd with only two small dogs. I really didn't relish the image of a retired couple with our two little pets. So we decided to find another large dog. Not a puppy. With all the stray dogs brought to the local SPCA, called the refuge here, we felt it socially incorrect not to adopt. My only demands were that it be large and female. I couldn't see Pinxo, the epitome of the alpha male, accepting another man around the house.

At the shelter, all the dogs were free to run around, bark, fight with each other and, in general, cause incredible chaos. They all seemed to know we were looking, and one after the other came over with a "please take me," look which made me want to weep.

"Don't feel bad," advised the dog lady, as I leaned down to pet a particularly pathetic specimen, "he's been here for 5 years. Never even one nibble for him."

I had my eye on a huge black, hairy mixture of heavens knows what. But J, as all men, was into looks. "We'll take this one," he declared without hesitation, pointing to a really beautiful, slim, long legged, short-haired elegant cross between a Doberman and some sort of mountain dog I had never heard of.

The dog lady informed us it was indeed a female, a hunting dog, and her name was Alias. She had been brought to the refuge as a puppy, was adopted and then brought back two years later when her owners divorced. I often wonder at the significance of her name or maybe it just sounded nice to French ears. She came with a very chic collar and leash. Obviously, her previous masters were well-to-do.

With Pinxo, it was love at first sight the moment we entered the house with her. He was in an agitated state for months after. Couldn't keep away from her and, although about a quarter of her size, spent hours trying to make love to her. Alias, cool and composed, just put her paw on his head. Finally, the panting and all the sex play really got to us and at the age of seven, Pinxo was "fixed." The vet warned us it might not change anything because the urge lives in memory. Pinxo did calm down a bit, but once in a while sex still rears its head. The friendship, thank heavens, is more platonic. Txonny hates Alias since with her arrival, she became the old lady in the harem.

Alias came into our life and into our home as a well-behaved, non-barking animal but it took about two months for her to pick up all of Pinxo's bad habits. Her main talent though was being able to reach up with her paw and open the kitchen door to let herself in or out. Somehow, we cannot teach her to close it, not that we didn't try. When we feel a cold wind blowing through the house, we know Alias has either come in or gone out. The urge to run is stronger than she is, not to escape, but for the pleasure of the gallop. She is as swift and elegant as a gazelle, jumps fences like a race horse and became a practiced marathon participant.

On Saturday mornings, when the local club of joggers comes through the surrounding vineyards, Alias takes off after them. Sometimes though she is the lonely long-distance runner, ending up in someone's backyard, lapping up their dog's water. She has been seen lounging around the local village café, at the tennis courts, or the skate board terrain.

Inevitably, would come the telephone call, "We have your dog" requiring us to discover all the unknown places of the village and surroundings trying to find her. I suggested to J that we should get her a GPS. These situations, however, are relatively easy, becoming more complicated when we received such a call at one in the morning at our son's house in Malaga, or on a bus in China. Thank heavens for cell phones and our very understanding *gardien* who was always ready to fetch her.

Alias is by nature a well-groomed dog. Short-haired and shiny, she looks like she just stepped out of a dog show. Reminds me of the girls behind make-up counters, smooth neat skin, every hair in place, who make me feel so imperfect that I decide not to buy that new miracle cream since there is no chance it will help. Like my two hairy dogs, I always look just a tat rumpled. The remedy for all three of us is the hairdresser. Mine is the local village guy who keeps me presentable. For Pinxo and Txonny, the beauty salon is a unique experience. It is a moveable feast, a small van run by a mother and daughter which makes the rounds of the villages.

Our village is on the Saturday schedule and the truck is in the parking lot of the supermarket. Space is very limited. Absolutely no room for dogs waiting their turn. But the two enterprising women found the perfect solution. The doggies are placed on a series of shelves lining the sides, which obviously makes quite an impression on them since even Pinxo didn't try to jump off. When I return to pick them up, they both have bows in their hair, Pink for Pinxo my macho male and purple for Txonny. They also come back smelling of Chanel Number 5 for Dogs, which temporarily makes Pinxo fall in love again with Txonny.

Once, jokingly, I pointed to J and asked *Madame* the canine coiffeuse, it she could trim him as well.

"We don't do pit bulls," was her response.

We do not have a doorbell, knocker, intercom or any other civilized way of announcing visitors. The three dogs set up a cacophony of barking when anyone approaches within a 100 meters of the house. This includes the *gardien* who passes by at least a zillion times a day. We used to rush down at the first sound of barking. Now we are much more discriminatory. If the barking stops within a few minutes, we know it is only the *gardien* walking by.

The only person they do not bark at, in contrast to the rest of the world's dogs, is the mail lady who comes by in her bright yellow truck each morning usually around 11 o'clock. By some incredible doggie instinct, they know it's her truck on the gravel and rush out to meet her. When necessary, Alias opens the kitchen door to let them all out. They rush over, line up in soldierly fashion and wait patiently for her to descend. Before putting the mail in the box, she gives each of them a biscuit. *Merci à la Poste française.*

When our vet opened his new clinic, it was a big event. We received a well-designed card in the mail inviting us for a cocktail and a visit to the new quarters. This promised to be the animal event of the season, so we wrote it into the social diary of the dogs. Only after careful scrutiny of the invitation, did we notice in the left-hand corner in very small print "no pets allowed." Alias, Pinxo and Txonny were, needless to say, very disappointed. They were so looking forward to snacks accompanied by a bowl of rosé.

We are sometimes blessed with four dogs, the addition being Rufus, a handsome Bouvier Bernoise, belonging to my son, who consumes more space than our three canines put together. Although closely resembling a Saint Bernard, he has, unfortunately, never been sent to us with a flask of whiskey around his neck. Whenever we are so lucky to have the pleasure of his hairy company, my son prepares him by telling him he is going to Club Med.

Rufus, in contrast to our three unworldly dogs, is extremely *mondaine*. He strolls in Aix-en-Provence without a leash, sniffing his favorite lampposts and has dined in some of the best restaurants. On the occasions I have walked with him on the Cours Mirabeau, he is continually greeted. "Bonjour Rufus." I get that "Who's she look." He does his best to accommodate himself to country life. Our three dogs regard him with disdain. He is in love with Txonny , a totally unrequited feeling. I think she should be quite grateful, seeing that she is old, deaf, not very beautiful and it's a now or never chance.

Alias and the hunters is an ongoing canine soap opera. Since she looks so much the part of a real hunting dog running through the vines, she is always being accused of various crimes by the hunters – scaring the pheasants, eating the partridges, bagging a hare and burying it for later leisurely consumption. Actually except for one incredibly small rabbit which was most probably killed by Txonny, she has never brought a trophy home.

Unfortunately, no matter what hour I choose for my daily walk with the dogs, we always manage to run into the big bellied, piggy eyed, moustachioed "*garde de chasse*" (guard of the hunt). He points a fat, stubby finger at Alias and starts to recount all her sins. "She eats the baby birds (in front of their mother) she tears pheasants apart, she scares baby rabbits."

"Good," I thought, "the more, the better."

And, he goes on, "I saw her in front of the rabbit cage of *Madame* Magnan." I had to bite my tongue to keep from asking him what he was doing in front of *Madame*'s rabbits since she has quite a reputation among the butcher, the baker and the candlestick maker.

On a Spring morning, the sky, azure blue, the fields gold with wild flowers, the Montagne Sainte Victoire a deep lavender, along comes *Monseiur* Piggy Eyes. "Bonjour *Monsieur*," I greeted him, sure that even a grump would be light-hearted on such a day.

"One day, I'm going to catch her," he replied, "and bring her to the pound. You'll see! You will get a big fine!" Alias regarded him with haughty indifference.

"Why are you poisoning my life," I asked disingenuously, "she doesn't hunt anything."

"I'm protecting the nature." And with that he stalked off. From Alias??

There came an abrupt end to the harassment of Alias. One day in autumn, at the beginning of the hunting season, Frederic, our wine neighbor, came to our kitchen door complaining that Alias had killed a hare. He had seen it in her mouth with his own eyes.

Seemed a little unlikely that Alias, admittedly a fast sprinter, could really win the race with a hare, unless it was the overconfident one from the fairy tale "The Tortoise and the Hare."

"So, where's the hare?" I inquired.

"Probably buried it," he replied. She would have needed a full day to make a grave big enough for a hare. But to keep peace, I apologized for Alias' indiscretion. But not my *gardien*! He was determined to find this famous hare. And he did. Sure enough in the garden below was a dead animal – a sort of large rat with a huge bushy tail – a *ragondin*, (coypu a large, useless rodent), two of which had been killed by Txonny and deposited on the stairs going down to the pool a few days before.

"*Voila*," said our *gardien*, dropping it at the feet of Frederic and his hunting pals. "Some hunters! Don't know the difference between a hare and a *ragondin*."

The real finale to the maligned Alias story came when Frederic's dog, Enzo, fell in love with her. He arrived on our doorstep one day, howling passion. Considering that she has long been "arranged," this seemed quite strange. But, to his credit, he is very discreet. Just nuzzles her or gives an occasional lick. Maybe he is fixed too. Occasionally, Alias rewards his amorous advances by putting one of her extremely elegant paws on his hairy head.

On a more serious note, hunters can be very dangerous and nasty enemies. They have been known to cut down a centuries old tree in the mayor's garden because he refused them rights to hunt on his property. Hunters poisoned our friends" dogs because they were scaring their quarry. Hair-raising stories about revengeful hunters abound. They have a certain power and don't hesitate to use it. Fortunately, our experience with disgruntled hunters has been limited to verbal abuse directed at Alias, who just shrugs it off with aplomb.

CHAPTER 7

OLIVES, OLIVES, OLIVES !

The symbolism of the olive branch dates from antiquity until today. Noah knew he was reaching land, after the deluge, when a white dove landed on the ark with an olive branch in its beak. Athena managed to restore a full-grown olive tree in one night to replace the sacred one destroyed by Perses. Conquerors were rewarded with a crown of olive leaves. Jesus entered Jerusalem on a road covered by the faithful with olive branches – a custom perpetuated until today in the ceremony of the branches. The Olympic torch is lit by an olive branch. The rays of the sun bouncing off a parabolic mirror ignite an olive branch, which blazes up and is used to light the torch.

We could easily have supplied all these branches. Just don't ask for oil. In the 25 years we have had this house with two lanes of 93 olive trees, not one has ever produced 93 olives. From time to time 5 or 10 shriveled up specimens fell to the ground, but the possibility of a harvest and our own olive oil was not an option. Until this year. Walking as usual with the three dogs along our olive lanes, with eyes cast down since this is often the poo-poo path if I don't get into the vineyards soon enough, I noticed a few olives. I looked up, and to my amazement, every tree was literally covered in olives. Now I know how those guys panning gold in the Wild West felt. I had struck green gold.

Olive trees are considered immortal. This is absolutely true. *Madame* Boulet had told us that in an extremely cold winter in1956, all the ones on our property froze, but not to death. *Rejets* (literally rejects) rose up in their place. These rejects form a new tree from the base of its deceased ancestor. It takes about 35 years for these offspring to start producing olives. Ours took over 50 but they finally came through in grand splendor.

Since they had never produced anything, except beauty, olive trees, even rejects, are gorgeous. We never did anything to encourage them, convinced as we were that they were sterile. No pruning, no watering, no spraying, no cajoling. Our tree-cutter told me, "Olive trees think." I can't imagine about what but maybe all the rain we had in the spring encouraged them to think positively.

J, who is totally allergic to any form of manual gardening, was thrilled to death with the sight of his major producing olive trees. "We'll organize an olive picking party. You know, all our friends, a great lunch, lots of wine. How many people shall we invite?" J uses the editorial "we" very often in regard to big lunches, dinners etc. He means me! "I'll take pictures. It'll be great." I didn't really expect him to climb into the trees but still I had hoped for a little more action than being the day's photographer. Perhaps pouring the wine.

Having never picked an olive in our lives, we really didn't know where to start. You do need some sort of equipment we discovered, such as; nets to put under the trees to catch the olives, a kind of special rake to comb the olives off the branches, high steady ladders since our trees were extremely tall never having been pruned, special cases to put them in. Absolutely no plastic garbage bags allowed.

Off I went to the local Agricultural Cooperative with my list, only to find out all the olive picking material was sold out. "Lots of olives," this year," my faithful co-op friend informed me. "Maybe in a week or two."

Since we had already managed to scrounge together 10 willing olive pickers for the following Saturday, that was not an option. You know who your real friends are when you ask them to come pick. Those with experience were all occupied with other important tasks, although they offered to come for lunch. Now that I have had the olive experience I can sympathize with their reluctance. It is hard, boring work no matter how much it is romanticized in all the books on Provence.

Fortunately, I managed to borrow everything I needed from friends who had just finished their own harvest. They were not into more picking, but I figured they deserved the lunch anyway. They also were great on advice.

Everything seemed set. I spent all of Friday cooking up a traditional *daube*, a kind of beef stew which brews for hours in good red wine, peeling tons of potatoes to go with it, buying great cheeses and baking four pies. The four pies are a major achievement for me. Don't ask how many crusts I threw out before I finally got those to roll out in some semblance of pie shape. All was ready, and we felt very much like Provence gentleman farmers.

Saturday morning I woke early, full of anticipation, ready to realize every expatriate's dream, looked out the window and regarded the black sky sending down more rain than we had seen in the past three months. It rained for the following four days. Into the freezer went the *daube*, the four pies and the potatoes, although I was told you can't freeze them. Too bad! I wasn't about to start peeling another five kilos. Before reassembling the troops for the following week, I checked the weather reports on CNN, BBC,

Orange and the *meteo*. (weather forecast at 35 cents per minute). The upside was four more pickers offered their services.

The day arose, blue skied and sunny. The pickers arrived in style for the job – some even sporting red bandanas, or broad brimmed straw hats. Fortunately, there was no wind to destroy this fashionista touch.

The nets were spread out so that several trees could be combed free of olives at the same time. There were lots of pickers. Everyone wanted to be in a tree, either on a ladder or climbing up the trunk. The olives poured down as steadily as the rain the week before. What was sorely lacking were sorters. Sitting cross legged on the slightly damp net, getting rid of the bits of stem sometimes attached to an olive (this is not good for the oil) and trying to avoid gathering up the leaves and small sticks with the olives when putting them in the cases, or fishing them out if they do get in, is not only back-breaking but tedious.

The sorters, including me, were in a state of olive-induced hypnosis and went about our tasks like robots while the pickers sang, joked and occasionally threw an olive at each other. Nobody threw olives at those of us on the ground. They fell with a thump on our heads at the sweep of someone's rake.

J, neither tree climber nor sorter – although at one point I saw him stretched out like a Roman at dinner, carefully putting olives into the case one by one – was the official paparazzi. He could use the photos for a book called "Olive Picking for Dummies."

Finally, it became close to lunchtime, so I had the excuse to stand up and escape to the kitchen to prepare the repast, praying that my defrosted food wouldn't taste of its freezer origins. Hoping for the best and counting on everyone having a ravenous appetite after all that physical work, I set the table, put out the food and went back outside.

"*A table,*" "Time to eat," I called out gaily. Fourteen vultures descended on the kitchen and devoured 12 hours of laborious cooking in 20 minutes. Even the defrosted potatoes were consumed with the same gusto had they been *foie gras*.

"Best meal ever," complimented one friend, an experienced foodie. "Absolutely delicious. How did you do the potatoes?" Undoubtedly, the unending filling of glasses by J enhanced greatly the appreciation of the food. Looking at the rapidly increasing amount of empty wine bottles, I had terrible visions of people falling out of the olive trees, combing each other's hair with the olive rakes or falling asleep on the nets as olives rained down on their inanimate bodies.

"Nespresso, what else?" to quote George Clooney. Lots of small cups of extremely strong espresso seemed to rev up the pickers and so began the afternoon session. I took my place with a few other sturdy souls and kept sorting, filling, sorting and filling until sunset. J, from his supine position, finally got the knack of putting handfuls of olives in the cases instead of one at a time.

At the end of the day, we had filled 10 cases, three huge burlap bags and 8 small crates borrowed from our local vegetable store. Numerous champagne toasts to the god of the green fruit were made, the booty loaded into two cars and off we went to the mill. Except for a few intellectually curious among our pickers who came with us, the rest went home undoubtedly to a hot bath resolving never to eat another olive.

Having no idea what to expect, we assumed you just dumped all the olives on some sort of scale and left. Nothing of the kind. First of all there was a line of cars snaking twice around the mill, all loaded with olives. What seemed unfathomable to me but I guess in line with French logic, the miller took those with the least amount of olives first. Those of us with serious quantities were asked to move our cars and wait on the side, while *Maman*, Papa, Jean-Pierre and Suzanne deposited their cute little baskets of olives.

Actually, it was a rather chaotic affair. Nobody waited in their cars. Lots of people were hanging out trading olive stories, including, J who proudly recounted the 50 years of bareness and incredible harvest of today. When I looked into the huge vans filled with olives of all sorts and colors from bright green to purply black, I wished he would stop bragging. Our olives looked awfully puny in relation to the round plump ones I was seeing in the vats.

To my great amazement and pride I found out later that those big round ones were full of water – not at all good for oil, in contrast to ours – short on appearance but evidently superior for oil.

With great aplomb, the miller managed to get the olives where they were supposed to be, weighed them and gave out certificates of weight. The law of olive oil is the law of 100. If you have 100 kilos or more your olives are kept in a separate container and you get your own oil.

At last, it was our turn. J pulled the car up near to the opening of the barn-like building. Vats everywhere, olives spilling out of some sort of conveyor belt being washed, pitted and made ready

136

for pressing. In the middle of all this action, stood an elderly *papi* (grandfather but also the French term for a real old guy) belting out the Provençal national anthem, *Le Cuppo Santo*, tears streaming down his cheeks. "He had a great harvest," explained the miller, "so he is very happy and thankful."

With wonderful professionalism, the miller emptied all our receptacles and began weighing our olives on an electronic scale, then dumped the whole lot in a container marked with our name. The computer spit out a certificate of olives delivered which the miller handed us with a big smile. "Not bad," he commented, "for beginners." We had picked 463 kilos of olives!!!! If you have more than 100 kilos, your olives are pressed separately, insuring that the oil is yours and yours alone. Nobody else's mixed in. Mutual olive oil is for those unfortunate enough to have less than 100 kilos to present.

"You can pick up the oil tomorrow," his wife told us. Unbelievable. I didn't dare to ask how much we could expect but of course J did. "It depends on your olives," he was told.

We found out afterwards, you usually count between 5 and 6 kilos for a liter of oil. The mill keeps a small percentage and charges around 80 Euro cents for turning an inedible fruit into a delicious green liquid. We were asked if we would like it in 5-liter *bidons* (jerry cans). Obviously not having any other option of transporting our oil, J nodded yes and was told these would be added to our bill.

The next day, as dusk began to fall, we headed for the mill, J with great assurance on receiving a huge quantity and me, with trepidations that there would be something terribly wrong with the oil. This is our usual half-full, half empty glass routine. The miller's wife greeted us with a smile and told us she would bring our oil to the boutique. "Just go in and have a look around," she said, "and we will settle the bill afterwards."

About 15 minutes later, she reappeared with 4 jerry cans, 20 liters, and vanished behind a plastic curtain into the mill. "What!" said J. "20 liters for all that work."

"I told you those olives looked puny," I replied with my usual pessimism. And then she came back with another 4 cans, and then another 4 and then still 4 more. Eighty liters of olive oil!

We went back into the mill to pay for the pressing and the jerry cans. The miller was holding a still-warm dead rabbit, a gift from one of his hunter clients. "Sometimes I get jam or eggs," he remarked laconically, dumping the rabbit into a basket."

"Great oil," he told us. "Totally pure. Just wait a few weeks for it to settle before using it. The color will lighten and the taste will be less sharp."

This advice we did not follow. Immediately upon arriving home, we poured one liter of the oil into an elegant bottle, tall and square with a gold cap, which, after looking all over for nicely designed bottles, I finally ended up buying at the Agricultural Co-Op. The oil, indeed was a very strange green color, slightly misty, but thick and unctuous. I got out some fresh bread, poured on the oil, sprinkled on some sea salt and savored each bite. True, it was a bit strong but for us it was nectar.

We invited all our pickers and sorters for a *degustation* (tasting). Maybe again, it was the influence of all the wine flowing or the fact that they had handpicked each olive, but the enthusiasm was overwhelming.

"French paradox," explained Victor. "Olive oil is why we have less heart problems than in America. Do you eat olive oil on your bread in the morning?" I had to admit to putting butter on my toast. "Unhealthy," growled Victor, "now you can change your bad habits before it is too late."

After sopping up incredible amounts of the green elixir, everyone got a bottle to take home, bearing an

139

extremely impressive label designed by Pierre – a photo of our house with the text "Chateau Vallat, *Huile Vierge Extra,* (Extra virgin oil), *Recolte* 2015 (Harvest) – as if we had been harvesting olives and making oil for the last 100 years.

Even after picking such an incredible quantity, there were still trees bearing lots of olives. However, since they were surrounded by all sorts of underbrush, it was impossible to lay down the nets. This thanks to our lack of maintenance all these years.

"Never mind," said my amateur farmer friend, Denise, "just pick what you can and make olives to eat." Anyone who has ever tried it knows you can absolutely not eat an olive directly from the tree. It really tastes awful besides probably making you deathly ill. "It's child's play," recounted Denise, "I will give you the recipe." When I hear that phrase, I already know it will be complicated and way above my culinary skills, but I am always willing to try.

PICKLING OLIVES
Pick 5 kilos of green olives. Smash them with a hammer on a board but don't crush them or break the pit. Just open them a bit. Put them in clear water to soak which you must change every day for nine days and heaven help you if you forget.

Nine days, not one less, not one more. On the ninth day, drain them. Boil 10 liters of water with 1 kilo of salt, some bay leaves, branches of fennel with seeds on the ends, a handful of coriander seeds, and orange rind. Pour this brine over the olives and put them in jars or a sandstone pot.

Six to eight days later, your olives are ready to serve with a glass of wine. Actually, it really worked although the ones from the market are still better.

Should one succeed in making the olives edible you can turn them into *tapenade*, a wonderful spread for toast at aperitif-time.

1 kilo of black olives

100 grams of capers

20 anchovy filets in olive oil

pepper

Put it all in the mixer until the consistency is spreadable.

Store in the refrigerator in a jar.

When ready to use, add a bit of softened butter

Note: Store bought olives work just as well.

CHAPTER 8

THE SECRET LIFE OF PLANTS

"Plants are like us," philosophized my *gardien*, Robert, as he cremated a large dead oleander, "they get old, sick and die." Oleanders are supposed to be resistant to almost everything except a freeze of arctic proportions. Evidently not this one, which managed to turn brown and wither for no apparent reason, requiring its removal and leaving a huge gaping space in a row of its cousins. Never plant things in rows, pairs or symmetrically. When one decides to go to plant heaven, you can spend weeks visiting all the garden centers and growers in the region trying to find the same species in a comparable size.

I, however, refuse to give in to Robert's fatalistic approach to plant life and death. I fight every sign of sickness with determination and fervor. I have a sort of garden bible which describes *ravageurs et maladies* (plant ravagers and diseases) in detail, with gory illustrations of half-devoured leaves, white powdered branches, curled up flower petals and all sorts of spotted and deformed fruits and vegetables. The variety of plant world afflictions is mind blinding. Reading my garden bible, I discovered that cabbages can have a hernia, that there is a malady *balais de sorcière* (witches broom) which attacks prunus bushes, and *pied noir* (black foot) which can be fatal to potatoes. And then, there are unseen sneaky sicknesses which destroy the roots of shrubs and trees.

Forever on guard for the first sign of ill health among the hundreds of varieties growing on our property, I will gather leaves with all sort of aberrations, compare them to the illustrations, look for the remedy and then check out the cure with the local *Cooperative Agricole.* (Agricultural Co-Op). This organization is mainly for the wine growers and serious farmers. However, since I have become such a good client, as soon as I walk into the midst of a lot of unshaven, overalled growers, I am greeted by the director with *"Bonjour Madame. Qui est malade maintenant."* (Who's sick now).

Aside from his professional advice, the group around is more than willing to offer a panoply of home-made remedies, mostly a lot less costly than the official medicines. These discussions can last for a half hour with each farmer determined to win my approval. I reward them with my most charming smile, lots of *"Merci Monsieur"* and buy whatever the co-op is selling.

We have a virtual medicine cabinet in our garage – sprays to annihilate a variety of insects such as *pucerons,* (aphids) *cochenilles* (cochenenil insects) *chenilles,* (caterpillars) *cicadelle* (leaf hoppers) and *araignées rouges* (red spiders); granules to put around the base of plants to ward off slimy invaders such as snails and slugs; grains dissolved in water to be poured around cypress trees with brown needles and so on. Then there are preventative medicines such as *bouilli bordelaise*, a sort of blue powder with which you treat oleanders before they start to show disturbing symptoms. Obviously, it didn't help the one now reduced to ashes!

There is also a plant hospital. Robert will burn anything blatantly dead but if there is the smallest sign of life he will do his best to restore the patient. Since I cannot abide looking at half dead shrubs, he will remove the offender and replant it in a special space reserved for such cases, well out of my sight. His success rate is about 99%. A few months later a healthy blooming specimen will be back in its old place.

Losing a tree can be a devastating experience, although I must confess in some cases I'm glad to see it go. Not so with a Florentine cypress, one of a pair next to the steps leading to the tennis court. Actually, there are two cypresses on either side of the stone steps going to the swimming pool area and two more perfectly aligned at the entrance to the tennis.

As I have warned, a pair of anything and, symmetrical as well, can lead to disaster. When the one cypress died, despite heroic efforts of Robert to save it, the only solution was to dig it up – a feat requiring 4 men –and banish it for burning. Since the four cypresses, planted 20 years ago were very high, well developed trees, how does one find a full grown, same size tree to replace the one missing? A tour of all the nurseries in the region and way beyond produced nothing – only pint -sized trees in comparison to the ones we had.

But sometimes lady luck appears unexpectedly. Our faithful plane tree cutter who had helped disinter the dead cypress came by one day. "I have a tree for you," he declared. I will bring it tomorrow. I need four strong men to plant it." A glass of rosé and some olives and he was gone.

One has to have faith. Never did it occur to us that the replacement cypress would not be perfect. Robert rounded up three other strong men who began by digging a huge hole to accommodate the newcomer. Our tree cutter arrived with an incredible beautiful tree. With our four strong, macho volunteers, and much huffing and grunting, a half hour later, the cypress was in place, almost exactly the same height as its partner. It is very happy in its new home.

The disinterment of the dead cypress and the replacement thereof was pragmatically and unemotionally accomplished. The removal of a huge lifeless conifer near our tennis court was another matter. Planted with a mate well over 50 years ago, symmetrically, it was well over 20 meters high. The two trees had grown reaching out to each other, causing them both to be rather lopsided. From one day to the other, or so it seemed, the tree on the right began to lose all its needles and turn a sickish shade of brown. Chopping down the dead tree was obviously a job for professionals.

Discussing this plight at a dinner party one night, my friend Elizabeth came up with a solution. "I have the perfect person for you," she said. He is honest, not too expensive, capable, reliable (not a quality in profusion in Provence) and works with a partner. They can do the job easily," she assured me. There were a few things she did not mention – like that he had converted to Buddhism, was very Zen and only worked four months a year, leaving lots of time over to meditate.

Two days later he arrived in the pouring rain, a tall, ascetic, read painfully skinny, young man with big, sad green eyes and hair down to his shoulders. He was soaking wet. I guess an umbrella was not nature's way. If it rains you get wet. J and I have other ideas.

We donned hooded raincoats, boots and a big umbrella and went down to show Alain our poor dead tree. Ten minutes of total silence passed as he regarded it with deep concentration. Finally, a long, deep sigh. "I hate to cut down a tree."

J with water streaming off his umbrella was rapidly losing his patience. "Yes, he said, "we too. But the tree is dead. And if you don't do this kind of work why on earth are you here?" J is not very Zen in these situations.

"Oh," said Alain, "I never said I won't do it but it is difficult for me."

"Listen," said J, taking a leaf out of Robert's book, "people get sick and die. They either get buried or cremated. We don't leave them lying around. Well, this tree has had its life, and a long one at that, so if you can't bring yourself to put it to rest, I'll have to find someone else." Very poetically put. Alain seemed content with this reasoning.

We returned to the house to discuss the nitty-gritty of price, timing and other such trivia, over numerous cups of herbal tea. However, money was not a subject Alain was particularly interested in. "It is not my purpose in life," he explained. "I work only enough to live at least 8 months a year freely. I follow the Dalai

Lama whenever I can. He is my inspiration. And nature. My partner will send you an estimate."

The estimate was hand delivered, post or e-mail not being a viable option. We accepted the amount and two weeks later the tree was gone, sawed into logs for the fireplace and the useless branches cleaned up and taken away. When they came to the house to be paid the agreed sum, Alain sheepishly asked "Are you sure it's not too much?" His partner who has a wife and child to support was less idealistic. "It's a fair price," he stated firmly.

"Absolutely, no question" said J and wrote him a check. That settled, herbal tea was served for Alain and me and a double pastis for his partner and J. A last note: the surviving tree is doing superbly pushing out in all directions. I guess it's glad to have a little space after being hemmed in by its partner for 50 years.

The care and feeding of flowering plants and shrubs, especially those in pots is a continual source of conflict between Robert and myself. In regard to watering, Robert's theory is less is more. Mine is even more might not be enough. This water battle goes on from May to September. He thinks plants should suffer to produce more flowers. I think they need to be spoiled with lots of water and expensive fertilizer.

After years of fruitless discussion, I follow the advice my father gave me for all situations. "Say yes, and do what you like." So, between twelve and two when Robert is having lunch, I sneak out, fill the watering pails and make the rounds. Sometimes I get caught, en flagrant, and am forced to make some sort of weak excuse like I was cleaning the mud off my shoes. This is an extremely feeble reason since I am either barefoot or in sandals. His look is extremely disapproving.

I am not a good gardener. My thumb is not green. But my will is indomitable. I read garden books like novels. The expertise gleaned from all this reading does not travel from mind to hand. But it does make it easier to tell Robert how he should proceed. However, I suspect he has my father's philosophy. He just does what comes naturally and mostly the results are successful. Especially the rose garden.

At the bottom of our property is a small walled in area which was once the *jardin de curé*, the parish priest's garden. Every grand house had such a garden to grow vegetables for family consumption. Summer vegetables were put up for winter use, winter vegetables eaten in the cold season, strawberries were turned into jam. Supermarkets were not the source of such foods. However, having had a few seasons of failed vegetable produce, even parsley wouldn't grow, I decided we should turn it into a rose garden. Vegetables can be gotten at the Wednesday morning market, but roses were my dream.

Robert marked off four rectangles and one square in the middle, used old railroad ties to make the border and proceeded to put in rose-friendly soil. We filled the middle square with red *"sevillian"* roses, a variety which produces scarlet roses from May to December and never but never catches any rose disease. I pored over catalogues, went to an incredible *roseraie*, where we waited for nearly an hour to have the privilege of buying roses – but what roses! Roses with stripes, deep almost black specimens, flaming orange roses, delicate yellow ones with pink edges, classic roses and those developed in the 21st century. I even acquired some from my friend at the *Cooperative Agricole* which he assured me were more beautiful, resistant and cheaper than any others I would find.

Robert duly planted everything, using his own color sense of what to put where. He added borders of rosemary, lavender and santoline, herbal plants, which are supposed to keep nasty bugs away from the flowers. There is a big apple tree on one side, providing shade and a hedge of lilacs, blooming violet in the spring, on the other. It is my corner of paradise. I have set there one chair and a small table. One chair to discourage visitors including J. It is where I go to read. Robert also loves our rose garden and spends lots of time dead-heading, turning the soil and, viewing the results, probably talks to them as well.

My good friend, Denise, is the most amazing gardener I know, considering her only experience in this field is having been the PR director of the Ritz Hotel in Paris. She and her husband left the hectic Parisian life and moved very near us a few years ago. The produce coming out of her rather small plot of land would make a New Jersey truck farmer envious. And she does it in her spare time, since both she and her husband found full time jobs in Aix-en-Provence, admittedly less stressful than their careers in Paris. Denise spends every non-working moment in her garden. I won't say puttering because it's too professional for that. The great ease with which she manages to grow everything in profusion is in sharp contrast to my failures achieved by enormous effort.

There's the usual array of Provençal vegetables —- eggplants, zucchini round or long, peppers in all colors and sizes, a variety of tomatoes I never dreamed existed – huge, tiny, round, oval, (I don't think she has managed a square one yet) fat red beefsteak tomatoes, vine tomatoes, yellow ones, even luscious purplish black specimens.

Beans of all varieties climb up aesthetic bamboo poles. She even grows melons from seeds she imports from California. Cauliflower both white and green, broccoli, turnips, leeks, cabbages, spring onions, winter onions, potatoes and a variety of salads arrive in abundance, in their proper seasons.

The fall produces huge pumpkins and American corn on the cob. Not to forget the tons of olives from one tree which keeps them in oil all year. I don't think Denise has bought a vegetable since she left Paris. When I regard Denise with wonder and admiration (and jealousy!), she modestly says "There's nothing to a vegetable garden except a lot of work. Really it's child's play." This seems to be the standard phrase used by anyone blithely giving advice on how to do what they can and you cannot.

Robert prepared a large rectangle and I bought all sorts of budding vegetable plants. Denise grows hers from seeds, but this is really too far out of my realm of possibility. We decided to start modestly, some tomatoes, a few eggplants, zucchini and mini peppers, nicely spaced out, with bamboo poles ready to receive the thrusting plants. We just badly misjudged the location of our vegetable patch.

Situated on the other side of the walled rose garden, slightly lower than the small stone wall behind, it was totally flooded after the first rain arrived three days after planting. Undiscouraged, Robert did manage some sort of drainage. But I guess drowning all those baby plants hindered their growth and everything came up after everyone else's garden had long finished producing. But what we ate was so delicious that the setbacks were forgotten.

A juicy round red tomato, still warm from the sun, sprinkled with sea salt and drowned in virgin olive oil with a piece of crunchy baguette is a worthy rival of caviar. The mini peppers were less of a success. I guess I didn't read the label before planting. They came out red and green, very beautiful. I cut some up into a salad and we needed an extinguisher to put out the fire in our mouths.

Zucchini were the one vegetable that arrived in a discouraging abundance. And if you don't pick them at the right time, they turn into baseball bats. How many ways can you cook one? It's a very boring vegetable and needs some jazzing up. Besides eating them at practically every meal and giving them as gifts tied with a blue ribbon, I still have a freezer full of *fantasie des zucchini* (zucchini fantasy). I think I must have spent days cooking, baking and sautéing them. I am still too new at having my own produce to let even one go to waste.

I will share some of my more successful utilizations of the green monster.

ZUCCHINI SOUP

Slice up four zucchinis, never mind if the slices are not even. Sauté in olive oil with a sliced onion (easier than chopping) and a diced potato. Add a liter of water, 2 bouillon cubes. Cook until soft, grate in some ginger and puree the whole thing in a blender or with a staff mixer. Mix in a spoon or two of *crème fraiche,* (sour cream) and serve topped with chopped coriander. Also rather good cold.

ZUCCHINI WITH CHEESE AND TARRAGON

Thinly slice the zucchinis, easiest if you use the robot. Sauté with some chopped onion in olive oil. Add salt and pepper. Don't cook too long – the zucchini should be a bit crunchy. Add two or three tablespoons of *crème fraiche* and a good handful of grated cheese, any kind, and lots of fresh tarragon. Put in a ceramic ovenproof dish and bake for about 15 minutes in a slow oven.

CREAM OF ZUCCHINI WITH CURRY

Chop one shallot, a branch of celery, and sauté slowly in about 2 tablespoons of olive. Add one grated potato, stir around a bit and cover with a cup of chicken bouillon – just make it from a cube, it works fine. Cook until the potato is soft. Pureé the raw zucchini in the robot and add to the potato mixture. Put in a cup of cream and at least 2 tablespoons of curry powder, more if you like it spicy.

All of these recipes are fast, easy and practically fail safe. They also freeze well.

Time and experience have improved the results of our *potager* (same old vegetable garden in French.). We changed the location to a higher terrain and Robert put in a state of the art automatic watering system, which doses the water correctly, avoiding flooding by an errant hose or total dryness through forgetfulness. We have dared growing some more exotic things like potatoes and onions. Each time I reach into my winter store of potatoes, admittedly not very well formed but delicious, I feel like a true farmer even if Robert does the really hard work.

I suppose grass can be considered part of the plant universe. You know the phrase about it always being greener in somebody else's yard. At our property it is always greener in all the places you never see – the area of the plant hospital, the field furthest from the house, the place where we burn leaves, outside the wall of the driveway. Never mind the care and love that goes into trying to maintain a decent lawn near the pool, a rustic grass field around the tennis or four small grass squares in our slightly pretentious *jardin a la française* (French garden), brown patches appear incessantly, weeds rule, rabbits dig, moss, although at least green, invades and kills the blades of grass. It is an ongoing war.

Admittedly, hot, dry Provençal summers are not very conducive to an English type lawn. Although I thought we had a very sophisticated computerized automatic watering system, given the price we paid, there are parts of the grass that never feel a drop of water except that which falls from above. Robert says the system is totally obsolete and the little valves that pop up to eject water continually malfunction. He has become a genius at replacing and repairing this antiquated system. Aside from the technicalities of the watering system, the soil is not made for lawns. It is *terre de vignes,* (the soil for vineyards). Indeed, you see a lot more vines than grass in Provence. Still we keep trying and the results if not perfect, and if you don't look too closely, are not bad. At least the total aspect is green.

Green is also the color of envy and boy do I suffer from it. Every time I visit someone's garden, I come home filled with jealousy over how much better theirs looks than mine. I've become so obsessed that I surreptitiously look around for weeds or yellow leaves or mildew on the roses just to make myself feel better. I have given up going on garden tours since I only come home depressed knowing I could never achieve this perfection. J suffers from none of this. He is convinced our garden is the most beautiful he has ever seen. He embarrasses me intensely by regaling everyone who visits with the tales of our fantastic, extraordinary garden. And funny enough, it seems most people agree with him.

CHAPTER 9

MAINTENANCE

As women go, I am pretty low maintenance. I wash away the grey myself, do my own nails, both toe and finger, am not into massages, facials or expensive beauty products since I have passed the stage of optimistic belief in miracles. One of the village coiffeurs, (there must be at least 10 in this small town. I have no idea how they all survive) himself bald, has a great hand with a scissors and manages to keep me in presentable condition. He even convinced me to put a few blond streaks in my hair. J was delighted. I think he secretly longs for a blonde wife.

I must admit though to a little bit of collagen in the deep roads between my nose and mouth. The decision to resort to this expensive and not painless intervention, as the French call it, came about after my son sent me birthday card with a picture of a Sharpie on it. "No insult intended," he laughed, "just a hint." The dermatologist who performs this cosmetic needle-pushing is totally wrinkle-free. J is no-maintenance. I cut his hair, trim his beard, and snip away ear and nose hairs for free.

Our house is another story. Yes, it is old, older than we are and like a very rich lady of a certain age, has a taste for extravagant upkeep. A legion of artisans is required to keep her looking like *la grande dame*. Paint peels, plaster falls from the ceilings, leaks spring, pipes explode, window- panes fall out. It is a perpetual battle against the march of time. Our responsibility is to see that none of this distracts from her beauty. Still, I have the feeling, the house is holding up better than we are and at our expense!

The first view to the world are the shutters, all 150 of them. Because of the blazing sun and the ferocious mistral lashing at the house, these need painting every five years. For the price of this facelift, we could probably buy an apartment in Paris. Such a project entails interviewing various enterprises, getting estimates and evaluating the promises they all make. Finally, we decided on a convincing gentleman who assured us he would send only his best painters, specialists in stripping and painting shutters.

He sent us four nice young men whom, I think, had never held a paintbrush in their hands but they were extremely enthusiastic. After the first disastrous day, I called for a meeting the next morning. I sat all four of them around the kitchen table, gave them a cup of coffee and laid down the law. If I saw one drop of paint on the floor, on the window- sill, on a plant in front of the house or in the garage where they took some of the shutters to paint, they would immediately be banished, and their boss not paid. Further each shutter would be as smooth as a baby's bottom or they would redo it until it was. That was the stick.

The carrot was, if they obeyed my orders to the nth degree, they could count on a coffee every morning.

The moment came to choose the final color. I must admit I am a bit maniacal about the exact shade. The chief of the shutter painters arrived one morning with the color he thought would be suitable. "Thank you for choosing for me but, no, I don't like it."

"*Madame*," he insisted, "it's perfect. Many, many shutters I paint in this color."

"Show me the color chart," I responded. "I'll have this one, this one, this one and this one. You can paint each shutter with one of the tones and I will decide."

"*Mais ce n'est pas possible.*" (It's not possible)

"Oh yes it is." I replied.

For 150 shutters, I was not about to make a mistake. He went off shaking his head, not very happy. The next morning when I came outside, four shutters had been painted. My painter stood there grinning from ear to ear. "Eh, *Madame*, which one do you like?"

"I will tell you at the end of the day when I have seen the colors as the light changes." "*Très bien,*" (very well) he agreed, "*Madame* is a true artist." He returned, and I chose the color. He seemed satisfied. The next day, his boss called and asked what I had done to upset his supervisor.

162

"What!" I screamed through the phone. "What are you talking about?"

"He came back tonight and told me he was so stressed that he cannot work for the rest of the week." was the reply. I guess he was the one with the artistic temperament. Maybe I should have given him a glass of rosé before he left.

In total contrast to the emotional disposition of our outside painter, *Monsieiur* Bardot our inside specialist, no relation to Brigitte but he is planning to look up his genealogical tree, hoping for some unknown cousinly bond, is the epitome of cool. "*Oui, Madame. Bien sûr.*" (Of course). "*Pas de problem,*" are his are his classic answers to everything.

When I telephone him to come assess the job to be done, a ceiling pocked by some mysterious leak, a wall shedding plaster like my dog in spring, or a complete redo of the kitchen, he comes immediately. This time it was the hall. "No problem, I will make it perfect. I will send the estimate or maybe I'll bring it myself, gazing into the last dregs of his pastis, "*dans la semaine.*" (week). He just doesn't specify which "*semaine*"– this week, next week, the week before Easter, before Christmas or before his vacation. *Dans la semaine* is an elastic concept in Provence. It can stretch on forever. Luck is with us. The estimate arrived two weeks later, hand delivered by *Monsieur* Bardot at pastis time. "I will start on Monday." We rejoice and empty the hall of furniture, art, rugs, everything. He arrives as scheduled, arranges all his materials, including a huge ladder, and vanishes, unreachable by phone, e-mail or carrier pigeon.

We pass off his stuff as an installation by a well-known artist. Since we do indeed have some far- out contemporary art, a few of our friends believed it.

Three weeks later, he arrives at 8 o'clock one morning, grinning from ear to ear and carrying an enormous sausage. "It's for you," he exclaims. "Comes from the Jura mountains. It's a great specialty."

Obviously finding any explanation for his disappearance superfluous, he proceeds to paint. And yes, perfectly. Not a drop of paint anywhere, everything smooth, asking me at intervals if I am satisfied. He even gives a coat to the doors and the woodwork, which were not included in the estimate. At the end of the week, the hall looks amazing, everything is cleaned up, and *Monsieur* Bardot helps us put the furniture back in place and hang the art. J gives him a double pastis for his efforts.

"Call anytime you need me," he smiles. "You know, I always come immediately. Bon weekend!" It may take a little longer than we would like but he does come and he does finish the job. A big plus here since workmen can just leave, with an "*à demain*" (see you tomorrow) and never be heard from again. When we decide to have the bathroom ceiling done, I must remember to ask him about his cousin, Brigitte.

Totally laid back and very pragmatic is our plumber, *Monsieur* Martin. He is large, rosy- cheeked and retired. As usual, it was Victor who sent him to us. He will only take on small jobs. No stress for him. But he is always available either to fix whatever is leaking or to advise Robert, our *gardien* on how he can do it. This advice is free and often comes coupled with the necessary tools. When something is particularly delicate, he will do it himself.

Lying under our old-fashioned sink trying to de-clog some ancient pipe, he looks like a huge bear.

"Putain! Putain!," he mutters when his efforts are foiled. This is a common expression among artisans in Provence. It literally means, hooker. I have never been able to get an explanation of the connection to venting frustration. Sometimes this phrase is replaced by *punaise* (tack) even more obtuse but politer. Other quaint expletives used when you bang your head or break your best crystal glass are mince (thin, like *elle*

est mince); zut – just the sound of it is satisfying; *mercredi* (Wednesday) or *crotte* (dog stuff).

These expressions are the polite versions of *merde,* the equivalent of "shit!" Why dog poo is more acceptable is another mystery of the French language. However, if it is not your own doing that sends forth these utterances, but rather someone really bugging you, *"Parle à mon cul, ma tête est malade."* (Talk to my ass, my head is tired) is a picturesque retort. Actually, this is not regarded as vulgar as I would have thought.

Monsieur Martin has an uncanny gift for finding the source of leaks, even outdoors. After three days of digging trenches in the lawn trying to find the one in our automatic watering system, Robert finally called for help. *Monsieur* Martin arrived, as usual bright and cheerful, regarded the furrows and asked Robert if he was planning to plant potatoes. "The pipe is broken there," he declared, pointing in the opposite direction to where Robert had been excavating.

"P U N A I S E!" cried Robert, the frustration pouring out of the word. Between the two of them, the guilty pipe was revealed and repaired with one or two *"punaise"* or *"putain"* enlivening the discussion.

After *Monsieur* Martin left, I told Robert potatoes in the middle of the lawn might be a bit misplaced, but we could plant roses. The next morning, the trenches were neatly filled in, new grass sodded, and the area roped off for protection from dog paws. The roses would have been a monument to defeat. Robert is very proud.

The trees and shrubs require another set of specialists. We have fourteen very tall and perfectly coiffed cypress trees. Unkempt, messy cypresses may be acceptable for new houses, like the "just fell out of bed" hairstyles in vogue among young models and movie stars, but totally unacceptable for our *grande dame*. Three times a year, Abdullah, the sculptor of trees, carefully snips away with ancient clippers. He has a perfect eye – hand coordination and each tree is exactly the same height, the same width and with nary a branch out of place.

He came to France from Tunisia thirty years ago as a young boy, finished school and has made his living ever since as a gardener. In fact, he worked for the old owner of our house, whom he adored although she never paid him. "Look at all the experience you are getting," she would tell him. "You should be honored that I have given you this chance."

Times have changed and now it is we who are honored that he keeps our cypresses in the stateliness they require – for a price. Abdullah is also a source of advice for the diagnosis and cure of any potential threats to our trees. We live in constant fear that one will, heaven forbid, die and require a replacement. Any disturbing sign like a few brown branches are cause for an immediate telephone call. He will proscribe some sort of magic potion, never just a manufactured product, and miraculously it always works. The advice is free!

Our terrace, covered in fine white gravel, is the size of a small village square and home to eight enormous *platanes* (plane trees), which tower above the house. They must be cut every three years to keep them from growing too high and scraggly. This is not a one-man job but requires a legion of fearless, dexterous young men who attach themselves to the trunk and proceed to saw away, hopping from branch to branch with the agility of monkeys. Suffering myself from advanced acrophobia, I am in a state of nervous tension the whole time they are here. On the contrary, they seem to be having a great time, calling out to each other, joking and laughing. I watch with sweaty palms.

Monsieur Garcia, the director of this tree cutting enterprise, is the son of Portuguese farmers, who came to France looking for a better life. The love of nature is in his blood. He started a small business of trimming trees and clearing woods and is now is the most famous plane tree cutter in the region. The trees in Aix-en-Provence and all the surrounding villages are in his capable hands. Normally he doesn't take on private persons but, considering the number of *platanes* to be cut, he considers us a corporate client.

Pruning plane trees properly is an extremely skilled operation. It is very important that the saws have been properly disinfected after each use to prevent the spread of disease from one tree to many. The art of cutting has changed with the times. It is somewhat gentler. Instead of radically cutting all the small branches, some are left as a *tir sevre* (pulling up the sap) so that the leaves appear sooner. Although *platanes* grow quickly, a meter per year, after they have been pruned, it can take until the middle of July before they give any shade. The *tir sevre* method guarantees at least a minimum of sun screen quickly.

Although he no longer climbs into the trees himself, *Monsieur* Garcia is definitely hands on, shouting instructions to his workers. "No! Not that branch. The one next to it. A bit more off on the right side. What are you doing? The branch is too long. It will grow through the living room window." And so on. Nothing escapes his professional eye.

Besides those in the trees, a few other men stand below loading the cuttings into an open-backed truck. This is no simple operation either. The larger branches are cut into fireplace friendly sizes and stacked for removal to our wood storage area.

Monsieur Garcia is very admiring of our trees. He advises me to talk to them. "*Platanes* need love" he says, "they are very intelligent trees." I'm a little too down-to-earth for this theory but I figure it doesn't cost anything to speak a few words to them now and then as I pass by and maybe it does encourage them to grow better. Who knows what goes on inside the trunks of these majestic beings.

Monsieur Garcia's other passion is *la chasse*. He has been a hunter since the age of 10. At the end of the job, he brought us two pheasants, in exactly the same state they were in when alive, with head, feathers and feet. With a big smile and a gracious merci, I accepted this gift of the hunt. Since my expertise in turning a complete bird into a meal is limited, as soon as he left, I stuffed them into a grey garbage bag and rushed off to the butcher, who, for a small fee, made them casserole ready.

And then there is Rémy, another of Victor's treasures, who keeps the property looking like Versailles. Almost two meters tall, he is a master of cutting shrubs into perfect round globes, trimming the high hedges completely straight and a decision maker of extraordinary confidence. He calls himself *tailleur sans peur* loosely translated – the fearless pruner. Without a qualm he will reduce a towering, albeit scraggly bush, to practically ground level or cut a lush branch to the core if he feels it disturbs the symmetry of a plant. Robert who anguishes about cutting ten centimeters from anything, except what is conspicuously dead, is horrified. I have complete confidence in my fearless snipper. Everything he reduces comes back fuller, healthier and looking very happy.

I did have one small criticism of which I informed him with great diplomacy. The place really was getting to look like Versailles, perfectly groomed shrubs everywhere, not a leaf out of place. I finally screwed up my courage and told him I wouldn't mind a few shaggy bushes, just for contrast. Now he alternates between the chic unkempt look and the strict. We still have an abundance of impeccably rounded shrubs but he has loosened up a bit.

Rémy has had a few wives and a couple of girlfriends since we know him, which does not surprise me. He is quite handsome. Recently, looking down from the scaffolding as he was trimming hedges he said, "I have something important to tell you."

"Oh no!" I thought, He's going to tell me he can't work for me anymore.

"I'm getting married."

With a great sigh of relief, I asked "When?"

"In September," he replied, "and I have something to ask you. Could we take our wedding pictures here? It's the most beautiful property I know." Considering the important role he plays in making it so beautiful, my answer was a heartfelt

"Absolutely." Talk about pride in your work.

And so, this demanding old house looks pretty good for her age, which to my great annoyance, is what my mother used to say to me. Like all kept women, carefully made up, she is best at night. With the lights dim, candles lit, flowers overflowing in vases and the table set with china and silver, she is quite seductive.

CHAPTER 10

NEIGHBORS

"Love Thy Neighbor" is not an adage much in tune with the French character and certainly not in Provence. In Holland, there is a saying, *"een dichter buur is beter dan een verre vriend."* (A nearby neighbor is better than a faraway friend.) This doesn't fly here either. More likely those next door are regarded as a better enemy than those too far away to hassle. Neighborly disputes arise over everything imaginable from property lines, water, roads, access, cats, dogs, parrots, figs, and even the smell of a pizza.

Our tennis pro, Victor, has been living in the same house for more than thirty years, as has his neighbor who lives a bit further up and is technically the owner of the road. The right of access in France is sacred. It is forever and cannot be denied. Nevertheless, perhaps in crisis mode because his wife had just deserted him for their plumber, he informed Victor he could no longer drive up the road to the entrance of his house. "You are ruining my road with your big car."

"Tu rigoles," (You've got to be kidding), Victor said upon hearing this piece of absurd news.

"Absolutely not. You can park on the main road and walk in or construct a new access on the other side of your property."

Obviously, Victor ignored this, using the same route as always, until one day when his wife was driving up to their entrance, the neighbor spit on the car. Victor's Sicilian origins are usually dormant but can surface when the occasion arises. He strolled up to the neighbor's house and rang the bell. The man came to the door regarding Victor with aggressive bravado. Victor fixed him with an eye that would do a Mafioso justice. "You ever do that again," Victor quietly told him, "and you'll be looking for knee-cap replacements."

Still, it turned into a court case, which lasted two years and cost Victor not only lawyer's fees but some mental anguish. It is beyond his comprehension that someone should behave in such a stupid, nasty manner. Although I am not a great believer in justice having once been told by a Dutch judge, "You may be right but that's not to say you will be judged so," I was delighted to hear Victor had won. The judge ruled that access to road could not be revoked and, moreover, all his costs, including lawyer's fees, were to be paid by the neighbor. When it was over, Victor just shrugged. "*Un fou.*" (A nut case)

Our personal trainer, Marie, whose family comes from Naples, also has southern Italian traits, one of them being a love of pizza. After all isn't Naples the birthplace of this delicacy, now famous worldwide?

Tradition rules that she must have an authentic pizza oven, which she had very professionally built by an Italian mason in her back garden. It was constructed to avoid trails of smoke blowing into the neighbors" yards as much as possible. In any case with its high chimney it produces less smoke than a barbecue, a general backyard attribute, prominent also at the neighbors.

Marie and Pierre, her husband, not Italian but still a master pizza chef, noticed every time they used their oven, the neighbor would turn up the volume of his radio to concert hall proportions. Pierre thought the solution might be to turn the hose over the fence and cool off this guy. But Marie, polite to the nth degree, decided to handle the situation with tact. She went around one day and asked what was going on with the radio. "I can't stand the smell of pizza," declared the neighbor.

"So how does the loud music help?" inquired Marie sweetly.

"Because it probably annoys you and you won't enjoy the pizza. Why don't you just tear down the (universal expletive) oven and build it ——— neighbors on the other side."

At the next pizza party, Pie of his band, specializing in

176

concert while he made pizzas. The evening was a huge success. Especially since the neighbor probably decided he preferred the wafts of pizza air to the live jam session. From then on quiet has reigned on both fronts. Marie still greets her nemesis with a polite "Bonjour *Monsieur*," but when he is out of sight her Italian genes come to the fore and she gives him *le doigt d''honneur* (the famous finger.)

My friend Denise, of chicken fame, has a do-it-yourselfer next door. According to Denise he lives alone and is totally charming, except he never finishes anything. He has a beautiful self-designed and built fire place, without a flue, thus unusable, splendidly waxed doors piled up waiting to be posed, shutters gleaming with new paint patiently lingering on the ground, an almost finished barbecue with a pile of bricks next to it and a myriad of other marvels cluttering the field adjoining their property.

"Ah, the field," smiles the neighbor. "I am going to plant an *oliveraie* (olive grove). Just wait, we will have gallons of olive oil. You and I will do this because I am so happy to have such nice neighbors." This has been promised for the last five years as the pile of works in progress grow in place of the olive trees.

But this is nothing compared to the dog drama. After Denise's chickens had been brutally murdered, she assumed the culprit was a nasty fox. Until one evening, she saw a big, black dog sniffing around the chicken coop and a light went on. She approached her handy-man neighbor to ask since when he had a dog.

"Oh no, it is not mine. He comes around sometimes and sleeps over."

"Well whose is he," demanded Denise, already extremely suspicious.

"He belongs to the *marchand de legumes* (vegetable vendor) in town," replied the neighbor nonchalantly.

The next day, on the pretext of buying some tomatoes (which she never does, having masses in her own garden), she approached the vegetable man with a big smile. "Do you have a big, black dog?"

"You mean Bacchus? Sure, he's mine."

Denise couldn't believe her ears. An orgy dog. Bacchus had feasted like an old Roman on her chickens, minus the wine.

"Your dog killed five of my chickens," Denise informed him.

"Really?" replied Mr. Vegetable. "No problem. I have insurance for Bacchus. They will pay you the cost of the chickens. The insurance is really very efficient. When Bacchus killed a friend's dog, they paid right away. Enough for them to buy a new dog!"

"*Monsieur*," said Denise evenly. "If your dog ever again sets a paw on my property, you will be the one claiming insurance for a replacement for Bacchus." She then went back and told her neighbor, no more sleep-overs for Bacchus or else!

Even beautiful flowering trees can cause neighborly disputes. Friends, Janine and François, living in the next town, have a gorgeous flowering magnolia tree, albeit next to the fence separating their grounds from the house next door. More than once, the neighbors complained that the petals were falling in their flower beds. They awoke one morning to find all the branches on the neighbor's side had been hacked off, leaving an ampu-tree.

François, an accountant by profession and reasonable and calm by nature, went to the garage, got out an axe, rang the neighbor's bell at seven in the morning and threatened to cut down every tree in front of their house. *Monsieur,* the tree hater, retaliated by assuring François he would poison his dog in return. The police were called, and, in true French justice, François was given a fine for menacing his neighbor.

Fig trees grow in our part of Provence in abundance needing very little human intervention. With or without much water, and in a poor soil they thrive producing luscious green or purple fruits. Figs can be eaten in a myriad of ways; drizzled with honey and warmed in the oven, sliced with *crème fraiche*, with soft goat cheese or drenched in a sweet white wine, but the most satisfying is right off the tree, sun-warmed. They can also be a source of neighborly contention when one has nutsy neighbors.

Our carpenter's wife is the local librarian, organizes poetry readings, has even initiated a foreign language book section and is by village standards or by any measure, a cultured person. Imagine her chagrin at coming home one day to find a huge paper scotch taped on to her front door with "*Vous avez volé mes figues. Je vous ai vu les manger.*" (You have been stealing my figs. I saw you eating them). Signed with a flourish by her next-door neighbor.

She was absolutely furious. Deciding revenge is as sweet as a fig, she wrote him a letter threatening to bring him to court for false accusations. Not a great threat since this would probably take ten years to settle in France. But that was not the point. She sent the letter by registered mail, knowing he works all day and would have to go specially to the post office and, undoubtedly, spend some time standing in line as

180

is customary here, to get his letter. No postman delivers a registered letter without a person signing for it.

Monsieur had the nerve to ring her bell and ask why she had written such a nasty letter, when she was the guilty one. "Listen," she said, "I wouldn't touch your figs if I were starving. They're shriveled up like your *couilles!"* (balls). Not literary but it sure made a point!

Our local florist is situated next to one of the numerous hair dressing salons in the village. Aside from selling parrot tulips and bird of paradise flowers, they have a parrot in a cage to add a touch of the exotic. The bird is not very bright and has never learned to speak a word. But it does have one talent – an ear-splitting wolf whistle. In the winter the parrot is in the shop and provides a certain amount of entertainment for customers ordering a bouquet. However, in summer, his cage is outside, practically next to the hair dresser and the bird gives out with his lecherous whistle at every female entering and leaving the salon.

Actually, since it is a unisex beauty parlor, the men get the same appreciation. The uninitiated turn around to see where the sign of admiration is coming from only to be regarded with the level eye of the parrot.

Not everyone is amused, least of all *Monsieur* Jacques, the hairdresser.

Politely, he asked his neighbor if he would be so kind as to keep his parrot in his own shop. "But why," asked the flower seller, "he loves to be outside and see beautiful women. Your customers should be flattered at being whistled at."

"By a parrot!" exclaimed *Monsieur* Jacques.

Some harsh words were exchanged. *Monsieur* Jacques called the police but, unfortunately, they could not find a law prohibiting parrots that whistle. Hoping it would scare the parrot into silence, the hairdresser acquired a cat. And indeed, the cat sat all day in front of the cage, gazing up at the parrot, who whistled on unperturbed. But I think finally both the hairdresser and the florist profited from the situation. The spectacle of the cat and the parrot brought an influx of customers to both businesses.

Neighborly revenge can take a subtle path. Gossip in a small village spreads like fire during a *mistral.* (howling wind from the north) This story was told to me by a most unlikely source, my rather aged and retired plumber, normally quite reticent about anything that doesn't concern the flow of water.

"Do you know *Madame* X?" he asked during a toilet- unstopping visit.

"Yes," I replied, "actually I do. Why?" *Madame* X is a rather attractive blonde, widowed and known for being super stingy.

"Elle a un oursin dans la poche." (She has a sea urchin in her pocket). Reminds me of some Dutch traits but on the other hand, the few times I have met her at a dinner or lunch, she seemed quite nice but, indeed, recounting all the things she managed to buy, or services rendered, for bargain prices.

My plumber continued, "Do you know how she pays the people who work for her?" Probably late, I thought but that is not so unusual.

"No," I answered. "How?"

"Well," said *Monsieur* Martin, rising up from his knees and slipping into a very secretive mode, "when they come with the bill, she invites them in, sits on the sofa, spreads her legs and says *"Payez-vous."* (Here's your payment). With that, he kind of blushed and went on deblocking the toilet.

I found this a bit odd, so I decided to inquire around. It seems she had been having terrible rows with her next-door neighbor because of her dog digging up his newly planted tulip bulbs. I suppose she told him what he could do with his bulbs. And he retaliated by circulating this scandalous story. She is very sexy and where there's smoke, there's fire but I haven't dared to ask any of my workmen if they have accepted payment. I do look at her slightly differently though.

J was also party to sexy gossip on one of his morning coffee klatches at the village café. A week or two after our olive harvest, J couldn't resist bragging about how much oil our olives had produced.

"Are you selling any," asked one of his cronies. J had to admit that it wasn't enough to start a local business.

"I just bought ten liters from *Madame* Lebrun," chipped in our local electrician. And that's not all I got, or could have gotten."

He went on to recount that when he arrived to pick up the jerry cans of olive oil at eleven in the morning, *Madame* was arrayed in a vaporous negligee. After loading up his car, he went back to pay her. "Please come in," she invited. "Sit down. I'll bring some coffee."

"I'm a polite man, so what could I do. She returned with a tray of coffee, minus the negligee."

"So, what did you do?" asked his buddy.

"I put the check on the table and ran like hell."

"Quelle mauviette!" (What a wimp) laughed his friends. *"Tu n'est pas un lapin chaud."* (Literally, you're not a hot rabbit).

"In America," said J, "we call that gift with purchase."

We too have not been spared neighborly dissent. Our neighbor, *Monsieur* Merlot (great name for a wine grower even if his wine is *Côte de Provence*) and owner of the surrounding vineyards has the habit of telling people, including the local bank director, that we live in the middle of his property. He fancies himself as le grand seigneur and we are the serfs. Indeed, the house and its four hectares of land is set amidst his vineyards.

At one time it was all one estate but the original owner, *Madame* Boulet sold off the vines with the farmhouse before we arrived, keeping the grand house for herself until we bought it. Actually, the vineyards have been sold and resold three times since we have been here. The present owners arrived ten years ago, fifteen years after us. I think our neighbors are just jealous that they have spent a small fortune trying to make a silk purse out of their sow's ear of a farmhouse and we have the true *château*. Château in Provence, however is a very loose term, used for the main house of a wine-producing property.

One day our *gardien* whose bedroom faces the road separating the two properties, asked J who owned this road. Actually, it is divided down the middle, one half belonging to us but with a rite of passage for both parties. "Why," asked J in all innocence." "Because," said Robert, "there are enormous trucks passing every morning at 4:30 AM. They go up the mountain on the firemen's road and come back loaded with huge stones. Not only do they wake us up, but the weight of those trucks is going to damage all our pipes and wires laid under the road."

J called *Monsieur* Merlot to ask what was going on. "We are going to plant new vines up there but first we have to dislodge all the boulders. And these rocks are worth a lot of money. We sell them to people in St. Tropez to use in their gardens."

"Your good right," agreed J, but why don't you go up the normal road from the village instead of behind our house?"

"Because the people along that road complained of the noise," answered *Monsieur* without a trace of embarrassment. "And it is forbidden to go up into the forest with trucks in the summer because of the fire hazard. This way no one is aware of it." As if this excuse was the most normal in the world. Never mind that he might set us all on fire!

For three days after this enlightening conversation, it poured. The trucks continued and the road behind our garage turned into a sea of mud. All the gravel we had so carefully placed was ground into the muck. We needed knee high boots just to open the garage doors.

Since we are not into denouncing, which we could have easily done by contacting the local fire department, I decided to take matters into my own hands. I have an old beat-up Peugeot 206, which, in fact, I love dearly but was prepared to sacrifice if necessary. I parked it horizontally on the road – at night. The next morning at 4:30 our phone rang. "Bonjour;" I said sweetly.

"Your car is blocking the road," screamed a very frustrated *Monsieur* Merlot.

"Really. Go around it."

"That's impossible," he raged.

"Go over it," I replied.

"Are you crazy? My trucks can't get though. You come out and move the car immediately." He was now fuming.

"Well," I said, "just use the other road. Or you could call the firemen to move the car. Oh, and one other thing, you touch my car and you're dead meat," *"viande morte"* but I am not sure if this has the same impact in French.

"Bon journée." And with that I went back to sleep with the receiver off the hook.

I left the car there for two days without any further word from my neighbor. Maybe they just decided to leave the rest of the rocks where they belong or perhaps he was afraid I would really denounce him. I like to think, he realized I was too smart for him. This is the most doubtful of the aforementioned premises.

J, who was very much against my rogue action, ended up being quite proud of me. He added a bit of fat to the fire and called *Monsieur* Merlot the next week to ask him to replace the gravel since we were really fed up slopping around in the mud. And to our great amazement he did.

The superiority of his position comes to the fore now and then. When he decided to clean out the underbrush on his side of our mutual border, he didn't bother to tell the workers where the property line was. Fortunately, Robert caught them just in time from demolishing a row of oleander bushes and some cypress trees on our side.

But I still believe in the Dutch adage. When we were invited to his daughter's wedding, we came bearing a beautiful gift.

CHAPTER 11

FIFTEEN MINUTES OF FAME

In the late sixties Andy Warhol proclaimed, "In the future everyone will have their fifteen minutes of fame." It's a prediction that came (too) true. A video on You Tube, a sexy photo on Facebook or Instagram, a provocative tweet on Twitter. Anyone can have his moment in the spotlight, a fleeting, soon forgotten, fifteen minutes of fame.

Our house has had a bit more, certainly more than its owners. It has been seen, and admired, by thousands of people across the globe. It has sold cars, underwear and dehydrated soup. A complete mail order catalogue of terribly unfashionable Swiss clothes, as well as a brochure of sexy men's underwear have been photographed in and around the house. The newest model of a Renault posed under our plane trees. Our huge abode has been the setting of several television dramas and lastly hosted a luncheon for owners of Maybach, one of the most expensive cars on the planet. The terrace was a parking lot for about 12 million Euros worth of automobiles.

We had often discussed ways to make this house pay for itself or at least contribute its share of upkeep. The most obvious was to open a bed and breakfast. With 10 bedrooms and adjoining baths, this was an easy option for J, who envisioned himself as an elegant host, pouring a rosé at the end of the day for his guests, while regaling them with the wonders of Provence. My take was quite different. I saw myself up at six, rushing off to the boulangerie for fresh croissants, getting the breakfast table ready, making beds and cleaning bathrooms because the maid hadn't shown up. Not for me

Our house's rise to fame and a very slight fortune began unexpectedly over a Sunday lunch in February. J and I had just returned from Ventimiglia in Italy and had bought all sorts of goodies – real *buffala* mozzarella, Parma ham, *parmigiano* cheese aged 100 years or so according to our very handsome Italian grocer, huge black olives, pasta made with truffles, sun-dried tomatoes and some great Chianti to wash it all down, homemade (not by me) tiramisu and limoncello for dessert.

We decided to break with the usual and sometimes boring traditional Sunday lunch *gigot* and go for the *cucina Italiano.*

One of our invited friends asked if he could bring a photographer friend who was staying with him. "He's a very interesting guy," said Jean-Pierre. "Does mostly fashion photography." Images of smoky-eyed beauties modeling unwearable clothes in French Vogue flashed before my eyes.

Christian, the photographer arrived, attired in artfully correct all black, barely got out a "bonjour" and began inspecting the house. "Casing the joint" describes it best.

"Perfect," he declared, snapping away with his small digital camera, all the while gulping down glass after glass of prosecco.

J was enthralled. "Would you like to see the garden? The tennis? The pool?" With my usual pessimistic take, I could only think he was planning a heist.

At lunch as he forked up my absolutely delicious truffle pasta, over which I had grated even more truffle and sprinkled truffle salt for good measure, Christian told me that actually his specialty was more commercial than artsy. His next assignment was a brochure for a French brand known mostly for men's sexy underwear, although they do make pajamas, robes and other masculine needs.

"I have been looking for a location," he said, "and your house and grounds are perfect. We will do the shoot in April. They are sending over a male model from California. Very surfboard type."

Why they needed to find a model in California and send him to our house in Provence to be photographed in sexy briefs is a mystery to me. Don't French guys surf?

"No problem," said J, not even glancing at me for at least a nod of approval. There would be three days of shooting, inside and out. "Don't worry about anything," Christian assured us, "You don't have to make lunch or anything like that. In fact we will invite you. It's going to be great."

After our guests left, I asked J if he had arranged a fee. "I'm sure they will pay us something."

"Yes, but how much?" I countered.

"All photographers pay for a location. They have a budget for that. You worry too much," was J's response. "You'll see, they will be generous." I think J's enthusiasm for having our house so sought after blinded his normal commercial instincts.

I had expected the photographer, the model and maybe an assistant. Instead, a whole football team arrived – 3 assistants, a dresser, a makeup girl, a hairdresser, a stylist, the account executive, a representative of the manufacturer, a very beautiful young female whose purpose I never did fathom, and six suitcases of men's intimate needs.

The male model was absolutely charming and always hungry. Needed a continual supply of bananas to keep his magnesium count up. But I did feel a little sorry for him standing next to our pool in the April chill wearing his very, very brief briefs. Somebody forgot to tell him Provence in April is not L. A. But I guess the thought of all the money he was being paid warmed him. He never stopped grinning. He fell immediately in love with our bichon Havanais, Pinxo, and insisted being photographed with him. Pinxo is mostly renowned for lifting his leg against our white couches and growling at everyone. But very Warholian, he was enjoying his 15 minutes.

Indeed, I did not make lunch but arranged a table in our local bistro. I didn't count on Californian health issues. Our model and two of the assistants were horrified at the menu.

"I don't eat meat."

"I don't touch paté, you never know what is in it."

"No salad please. Can't trust the water used for washing it in foreign countries."

"*Poulpe?* What's that? Octopus. Oh my God!"

The Provençal waiter looked at them as if they had just landed from Mars. I finally ordered them a plate of grilled vegetables, "without fat, please." The

French contingent ate up a storm of forbidden food. J and me too. After all, they were paying.

The gorgeous surfer hulk never lost his good humor. He posed on the couch, casually clad in a robe falling open to reveal his blonde chest hair, Pinxo curled next to him. He didn't complain about the cold standing next to our fish pond in his black sleeveless undervest, black shorts and black socks. Propped up on our bed, now made up with black satin sheets, he pretended to read a copy of the local "*La Provence*" newspaper, attired in white silk pajamas, his blonde curls properly tousled. All these "informal" shots took hours of preparation before the camera clicked.

For three days we lived in the glamorous world of a fashion production. Jules loved every minute of it, taking his own photos. I was glad when they left. They thanked us profusely and promised to send us copies of the catalogue. They even bought a new collar for Pinxo, rhinestone studded. "So, what are we getting paid?" I asked J.

"Well, I didn't really discuss it but I'm sure we will receive something in the mail. He was right. We did. Three black mini briefs, 2 pairs of black knee socks and a black bathrobe weighing about twenty pounds. The briefs and the socks went to our son. I think the bathrobe is still buried away in a closet somewhere.

We learned our lesson, or at least J did. Negotiate the price beforehand.

But the career of our house was launched. A few months later, we received a call from a very good friend in Paris. "Hey, did I tell you I changed jobs. I'm now doing the advertising for a well-known brand of dehydrated, packaged soups."

Charles' enthusiasm for the gourmet taste of these soups when dissolved in boiling water was a bit beyond me, but my ears pricked up when he said he was looking for a location for two 60-second TV spots.

"Your kitchen would be just the right setting. Are you there on Thursday? I'll send my assistant down for the *repérage*."

I pride myself on my French vocabulary, but this word sent me straight to my French – English dictionary. It means location and in this case scouting the location.

A very young and very bearded man appeared at our door Thursday morning, armed with an impressive digital camera hanging around his neck. "I'm Louis-Simon," he announced, giving both J and me a handshake, accompanied by a bear hug. Running his words together as the French are inclined to do, it sounded to me like Louissimo, a French version of the Italian Massimo.

"Your kitchen is *magnifique,* much nicer than the other ones I saw today." J and I looked at each other. Obviously, we were not the only candidates. But J sprung right in telling our *repérager* that not only was our kitchen fabulous but perfect for filming. Lots of place to park trucks with equipment on the terrace, easy access, beautiful light and if they needed extras, we could supply three dogs

Louissimo was in and out in 15 minutes (not of fame). "On to the next kitchen. Two more before I get the plane back to Paris. Makes 8 today but yours is the most beautiful." I thought, "I bet he tells that to all his kitchen prospects."

"Isn't that great," exulted J, "another job for the house." His optimism never ceases to amaze, and annoy me.

"What makes you think they'll pick our kitchen," I asked.

"Because it is the best," replied J coolly, pouring himself a pastis.

Three days later Charles phoned. "The client loves, loves, loves your kitchen. We'll be there two weeks from today."

"Great," said J, "how much are you paying."

"Well, we will probably only need a half–day so, maybe 300 Euros."

J is a fast learner. "We don't do half days. Multiply by 5 and you can have a whole day. And it is a special price because you are a friend." J was not about to be paid off in packages of dried soup!

It seems a soup commercial does not need quite as large a retinue as men's underwear, although there were more actors and actresses, albeit not very glamorous. There was a rather ordinary young woman playing the mother, two cute kids, a boy about 7 and a girl 9, and a very round, rosy cheeked, middle aged man, the gourmet chef.

Much more equipment is necessary for a film than for still photography. A huge truck parked on the terrace spilled out wires, cameras, lights, sound equipment and some other stuff I couldn't quite identify. And baskets of vegetables; zucchini, carrots, string beans, celery, onions, parsley and an incredible amount of mushrooms.

I concluded there were to be two kinds of soup, one vegetable, the other mushroom. All absolutely home-made by *maman*. The baskets of vegetables were the silent stars of the film, with our chef now dressed for the part with a white chef's hat, checked pants and a very elegant chef's jacket. There he was, in our kitchen, peeling all these vegetables, smiling for the camera.

"Only the best, and the freshest, for my vegetable soup." Cut to a table (ours) now decked with a red and white checked table cloth and two adorable children, properly sitting straight up as French children are taught to do, spooning soup into their mouths as mommy proudly looks on.

"C'est si bon," (so good) says little Gaston.

"Délicieux, maman," (Delicious mama) echoes adorable Chantal.

In an aside, *"Merci, Chef,"* says *maman* to the chef-dressed man in the background.

This scene was repeated about 10 times before the art director was satisfied that the inflection of the voices, the facial expressions and heaven know what else were perfect. They then went on the mushroom soup. Except for a huge basket of mushrooms in the middle of the table, now decked out in a blue and white check cloth, the scenario was pretty much the same. In between shots, the children laid down on the dogs' couch, snuggling and petting them. They were in heaven – dogs and kids.

By four o'clock it was over. Everyone was very enthusiastic. The producer promptly wrote out a check and told us to keep all the vegetables. Much better than the packages, I thought. I had fresh vegetable and mushroom soup for weeks after. I didn't dehydrate but did freeze quantities. At dinner parties, J exulted in telling the origin of the soup and exhorted our guests to watch for the TV commercials.

J decided our house was becoming a professional and all professionals have a portfolio of photos to entice prospective clients. Although he considers himself a fantastic photographer, he decided our house needed a highly skilled photographer to do justice to its many possibilities. He decided to call Christian since he figured he owed us one after paying off three days of location with some underpants.

"Why would he do it for free?" I asked.

"Why not," responded J. "Maybe he wants to use the house again. I can always ask." I should have known. What J asks for, he usually gets.

Christian was delighted to come. "I am going to be in Aix next week. So glad you called. Are you doing lunch? Actually, I have an assignment from a Swiss mail order house and I was thinking of your property. They want a Provençal atmosphere. And you have those great *platanes*."

He agreed to photograph the house, the property and anything else we wanted. And, of course, we would be paid by the Swiss. "Just name your price. They have loads of money."

The Swiss may have loads of money in those numbered accounts, but they don't give it away easily. Christian and the client arrived a week later, a very Heidi type lady with a Swiss -German inflection in her rather picturesque English. "Ja, ja," she said. "Beautiful house." That was the extent of the pleasantries. From then on, it was down to business.

J had met his match. They both could have had a stall in a souk in Morocco. I went into the kitchen for a tray of rosé and some toasts covered in *foie gras*, hoping to calm down the bargainers. Heidi devoured the toasts, drank a half a bottle of rosé and struck her deal with J.

"I pay half of what you ask. Good, ja?"

"Very, good," answered J. "Because you are so charming, I will make a special price." Smiles all around. J had asked such an outrageous sum, that the half was more than he had ever dreamed of.

A month later on a beautiful spring morning, two caravans pulled up on our terrace. The Swiss are organized. Everything they needed, including the models, was in those two vehicles. The clothes were on metal racks and only had to be unloaded and wheeled into our green house, which would be used as a dressing room. Three makeup tables followed. Cameras, lights and a white screen came out. A refrigerator filled with soft drinks and water was installed.

They had even brought their own toilet paper!

The company specialized in attire for –to put it politely – the full figure. These really awful clothes were being photographed on models only slightly more padded than their anorexic colleagues. Even fat mail order clients want to be seduced into thinking the clothes will turn them into the models.

Everything was smooth and efficient and totally boring especially since conversation was difficult, our Swiss German not being up to par. The appearance of Heidi livened things up. She pronounced everything *"wunderbar*,*"* spent the day sipping, maybe not exactly sipping, glass after glass of rosé with her drinking partner, J. She invited us and Christian to dinner that night. The rest of the crew were left to fend for themselves.

No health issues for Heidi. She chose one of the best restaurants in Aix-en-Provence specializing in true French cuisine – lots of cream and butter, *foie gras,* veal with *morilles* (a very expensive black wild mushroom) and an array of the richest desserts known to gourmets. Without even asking, she ordered for us all, in surprisingly good French. Champagne to start with and an incredible Chateau Latour Pauillac, 2010 were commanded. One bottle barely lasted through the first course. Another was immediately requested.

With a glass of Moet et Chandon in her hand, she toasted "the most beautiful house in Provence" and began the story of the firm of which she was now president.

She told us her father had started the business in the 70's to bring "fashionable clothes" to women living in the provinces by mail order. He did a quick personal market survey and discovered that his potential clients were not a size 6. Such a niche in the market offered a great opportunity and he decided his catalogue would cater to the well-rounded Swiss "frau."

He put together a small range of outer apparel in large sizes, designed hopefully to camouflage the extra weight, as well as a line of intimate apparel including bras in cup sizes at the end of the alphabet. Heidi was a walking advertisement for her product.

Her father had retired at the age of 80 to pursue a new career as a pianist, leaving his daughter in charge of the now multi-million Swiss Franc business. "I do the fashion part," explained Heidi, "and the advertising and everything else creative. My brother is in charge of the financial side. He has no imagination and is a very boring Swiss man but good with figures. Ha! Ha!" she laughed. "Financial figures, only. Also, his wife is very skinny and can't wear our clothes, like you," she said looking at me. It didn't sound like a compliment.

Heidi left the next day as suddenly as she had appeared, leaving a check for three full days. We never heard another word from her nor did we receive a copy of the catalogue. I guess she figured it would be wasted on me.

True to his word, Christian sent us a CD with fabulous photos of our house, inside and out. He had even photographed the three dogs, alone and together, in the event canine extras might be required. J took on the furthering of our house's modelling career with the same zest if he were promoting Claudia Schiffer. He had me copy the CD twenty-five times, enticed a designer friend to make the cover for the case and wrote an advertising blurb so outrageous I blushed reading it. The CD was sent to location agencies all over France. J decided to keep it local for the present. European expansion would follow.

"We'll be very choosy whom we pick," said J.

"Yeah, right," I thought. We'll be lucky if anyone reacts. "

In fact we had three responses. The first to telephone asked how many beds we had and if they were king size.

J naively asked, "Are you planning to photograph sheets?"

"No," replied the voice on the other end. We are looking for locations for 'adult art movies'."

"Not in my beds," J said as he slammed down the receiver. "What a nerve!" he fumed, recounting the conversation.

"They do pay well," I said. I couldn't stop laughing. All that work and what do we get – a proposal for a porno film.

A few weeks later though, we had appointments with two serious contenders. Both were for using the house and grounds for a TV film. The first to come, a long haired, long legged and long nosed young woman carrying the biggest Louis Vuitton bag outside of luggage I had ever seen. She poked her oversized nose throughout the house, inspected the garden and pronounced it all "not suitable," got into her black Smart and disappeared in a cloud of dust.

Two days later we received a group of four people looking for a suitable location for a TV movie, the producer, the script writer, the decorator and the cameraman. J in his guise as our house's agent took them through the house, all over the property, praising the virtues of such an exceptional venue. They were properly impressed and decided on the spot that they would do four days of shooting. I retreated to the kitchen for the usual rosé and olives when J went into haggling mode.

The film was to in four parts to be sent out during the summer – *un feuillton d''été* . Usual summer fare. The intriguing title was *L'Eau Trouble* (Troubled Waters) and starred a very well-known actor of cinema and the *Comedie Francaise* of whom I had never heard. Maybe he sensed this, since after the first "*bonjour*," we never exchanged another word.

In fact, there wasn't much communication with any of the participants of this movie set. There were myriad people; camera men, sound specialists, makeup artists, assistants and their assistants, electricians, gofers and several comediennes, as actors are called here, even when they are not being funny. Except for a few questions like "where's the toilet?" there wasn't much conversation. They regarded us as invisible, except for the time when the command "Silence!" rang out and one of our dogs barked.

The guilty dog, Pinxo, was severely reprimanded and we were told in no uncertain terms we were responsible for keeping our animals quiet. Such disturbances during a shoot were totally unacceptable. I can't explain it myself but from then on every time the word silence was called out, the dogs stopped in their tracks, stood perfectly still and quiet until the all clear sounded. Absolutely amazing.

Apparently, the *Monsieur*, Michel Duchaussoy, unknown to me, was quite famous. J questioned some of the assistants who spent a lot of time just hanging around waiting to render some important service, like getting a cup of coffee or a Kleenex, and found out he was renowned in France. J, whose PR genes rise to every occasion spent a lot of time talking with M. Duchaussoy.

"What for?" I asked.

"You never know," replied J.

"Are you planning to produce a play?" I asked rather sarcastically. J just shrugged and went over with two glasses of wine and soon was engaged in a very deep conversation with his celebrity.

The shooting finished on time. The producer gave us a check, thanked us, patted the dogs and left the lower echelon to pack in. "Wasn't that great!" marveled J. "Oh and Michel invited us to see the play he is doing in Paris. I just have to phone him to say which night and he will reserve VIP seats for us."

Actually, we never did go to the theatre. We did watch the TV serial until we saw the role played by our house. The rest was just too boring.

Our house's next gig was top secret. It was to be the location for a photo shoot to introduce a very upscale, chic and expensive French automobile. We were not even told the make of the car. It would take two days and no visitors would be allowed on the property.

We had to sign a very official looking contract agreeing to this. For what they were paying we could limit our social visits for two days. The view on the Sainte Victoire and a huge platane on the terrace seemed to be the aura they were trying to get across.

The car was towed in, wrapped in a grey shroud, after dark. It was accompanied by the photographer, the advertising agency account executive and a burly man who would guard this treasure through the night. Fortunately, it was summer.

"We will start tomorrow at 7, need to take advantage of different aspects of light," said the photographer. "Is this all right with you?" Money is a great alarm clock. We were up early bright eyed and bushy tailed. Exactly at 7 we stood ready to greet our guest.

The car was not unveiled for another two hours when all the equipment had been set up and the models had arrived. No sleazy half-dressed girls for this car. Rather an extremely elegant couple. Both totally dressed in white. The woman had on a sleeveless white dress, an enormous brimmed white straw hat and white gloves up to the elbows.

Her partner, very Gatsbyian was dressed in a white linen suit with a white silk handkerchief tucked in the breast pocket. The auto when the shroud was removed was midnight black. It all could have been a Cecil Beaton photo.

Our alpha male, Pinxo, decided to claim the car as his own by peeing on the front tire. The cries that arose from the crew were deafening. Two assistants came dashing over, one with a bottle of Perrier and the other, more realistically, with one of our watering cans. Pinxo was banished to the garage for the rest of day.

The car was moved all over the terrace, from one tree to another, in front of some flowering shrubs, at a point where the Sainte Victoire looked its most spectacular. Each new location required at least an hour to set up the equipment, dust the car off, and check the models' makeup and hair. I was quickly bored and retreated into the house to read. J took his own photos. No one seemed to mind.

The high point of the day was lunch. A truck arrived with tables and chairs, gourmet sandwiches and, as befitting such a chic auto, several bottles of champagne. We were invited to the repast. The models changed into jogging clothes. No one was taking chances on a wine speck on their pristine white outfits.

They were very decorative additions to lunch but talked only to each other. In contrast, the photographer never shut up. He was specialized in photographing autos and had done advertising campaigns with every vehicle from the new Fiat 500 (color pink) to Ferraris, both vintage and new. Despite coming in a steady stream, his tales were fascinating. J, whose interest in cars is less than minimal, sought out the account executive in a campaign to promote his client (our house) for further roles.

Months later when the advertising campaign was launched, we saw the photos in Vogue. They were truly spectacular. Our verbose photographer had captured the light reflecting the shiny black surface of the car, the white clad models and a glimpse of the majestic mountain.

Our next car proposal was not for an advertising campaign or for a TV spot but for a luncheon for 24 owners of Maybach. For the less initiated in auto lore, which includes us, the Maybach is probably the most expensive car on earth. Made by Mercedes in Stuttgart, it was the favorite of Hitler. Not the best reference. This was probably the last of such excursions. Maybachs are now out of production.

Stripped bare, it costs about 500,000 Euros. Equipped and personalized, the only way a Maybach client wants it, runs around 1,000,000, more, I suppose, if you want gold handles.

This all came about thanks to our friend Elizabeth, whose husband, Christian, was the French consul general in Stuttgart. Each year, Maybach invites a group of their clients to a super-deluxe, over-the-top trip befitting the status of such people and their cars, all expenses paid. Only the very rich manage to get such freebies. This year, Provence was the destination. They would be lodged in the best hotels in Nice, Cannes and St. Tropez, taken to all the Michelin three-star restaurants and left lots of time to accumulate all the goodies of Louis Vuitton, Dior, Gucci, Prada, et al that the Cote d'Azur has to offer.

But they wanted a real Provençal experience. The director of Maybach, a good friend of Christian, asked for suggestions. "Of course, *mais oui, mais oui*, Elizabeth will prepare a typical Provençal lunch at our house." Christian is always enthusiastic if not always realistic.

The road leading to their house requires a jeep not a Maybach. Elizabeth called me in a panic. Could she use our house? She would arrange an aperitif at the pool, organize the lunch with the help of her nephew, a budding chef, set and decorate the tables and hire people to serve. And we would be paid just for hiding upstairs in the bedroom. Well, that is not exactly what she said. It's what we assumed.

The day before, Elizabeth arrived with the organizer from Maybach in their car. I thought it a rather mundane looking vehicle, a relative of Mercedes who manufactures it. I am sure it has wonderful hidden technical qualities but for that money I would prefer something flashier – a red Ferrari for instance.

The representative took a quick look around, seemed to find everything to his liking, refused a glass of rosé "I am driving a million Euro car, can't risk it" and left. Elizabeth called later to say he was more than satisfied with us.

On a beautiful Spring day, precisely at 12 noon, twelve chauffeured Maybachs arrived on our terrace, parking in a semi-circle for all to admire and disgorged a motley crew of passengers. Indians, Chinese, Japanese, Dutch, German, Swiss, English – all in an array of fashion, from grunge to Gucci.

But instead of peeking surreptitiously from an upstairs window, we were on the front steps surrounded by our dogs offering our hands with charm and grace to our guests. Fifteen minutes before they arrived, Elizabeth informed us she really hated playing hostess on these kinds of occasions. She would remain backstage in the kitchen and we would have the dubious honor of playing the role of Duke and Duchess of the chateau –American style.

J was delighted and felt he was absolutely perfectly dressed in his oldest jeans and purple t-shirt. I quickly ran upstairs to change into my most suitable Zara dress.

The first couple we greeted were from Hong Kong, she tottering on 6 inch Manolos through the gravel on our terrace. "Very nice," she said. "How much does it cost if I want to buy the house? 24 million Euros?"

J looked at me with a tell her to write a check NOW expression. "Maybe I'll just rent it." I smiled sweetly and told her champagne and hors d'oeuvres were awaiting her at the pool.

Elizabeth with the help of her nephew caterer had prepared a sumptuous feast. There were flowers everywhere, a huge Parma ham waiting to be thinly sliced, mounds of fresh shrimps, oysters nestling in ice in a wooden boat, tiny glasses of cold gazpacho, little meatballs, hot and spicy, beautifully cut carrots, radishes and celery waiting to be dipped in a garlicky guacamole and myriad bottles of champagne in a huge silver container filled with ice.

The hungry hordes of some of the richest people on earth descended on the feast as if they hadn't eaten in days. Except for the Japanese couple who were too busy photographing everything in sight –especially our dogs who, for a meatball or piece of ham, posed gracefully.

Inside, the tables had been splendidly set with a spring theme by Elizabeth. A rectangular table in our entrance hall, not to brag but it is the size of a huge dining room, was covered in a beautiful green tablecloth bought by the meter at the market and not even hemmed, only knotted at the corners. Two glass bowls mounted on thin-stemmed bases, filled with green peppers and yellow daffodil heads, spilling over with ivy, were at each end of the table. This decoration, well thought out by Elizabeth, was just tall enough so as not to block cross conversation.

In the dining room our table, actually just a huge round board on saw horses, was covered by a yellow floor length market cloth, disguising its humble origins. The same bowl, this time in the center of the table, contained masses of lemons and their leaves.

J hosted the green table. His guests were Chinese, Indian, Indonesian, Korean and South African. He accumulated lots of business cards and invitations to come visit. English was the mutual language. The Chinese were rather silent. Chopsticks were not available.

My table was European except for a Japanese couple, she looking about 15 and absolutely gorgeous, he, elegant, grey haired and probably on the wrong side of 60. On my left was an enormously fat German man accompanied by his wife of equal girth. During the first course, grilled scallops with mango chutney, he confided to me that his only joy in life was his Maybach. "My wife hates me. She's waiting for me to die so she can have all the money." The things perfect strangers tell you! He drowned his sorrows in a glass of a Bordeaux grand cru.

On my left was a Dutchman, only slightly slimmer. When I started speaking to him in Dutch, he grinned from ear to ear with undisguised happiness, leaned over and gave me a peck on the cheek. His Dutch accent was pure working-class Amsterdam, the equivalent of a Cockney Londoner. He obviously did not come from the upper echelons of Dutch society.

I was curious how he had become wealthy enough to buy not only one Maybach but two. He told me that at age 10 he was already working the rides at a fair which came twice a year to his neighborhood. "It was the Ferris wheel I loved." And that was to be his future. He was the one who set up the huge Ferris wheel in the Tuileries in Paris and from there in cities all over the world.

"But how did you manage to convince the French authorities to install such a huge thing in the sacrosanct Tuileries?" I asked.

"Chirac (the former president of France) likes me," was the reply. No further explanation. "You speak wonderful Dutch," he said. "I am so happy to sit next to you." And then whispered in my ear, "Such snobs all these people." Actually, he said it in Dutch, which comes over a little less polite and more forceful.

The main course, succulent lamb, slowly simmered for at least seven hours in true French tradition, came with a bouquet of miniature vegetables tied together with a strand of chive. Except for the Japanese girl who ate two small carrots, everyone else including me gobbled it all up, washed down with the best wine from our neighbor's vineyards.

La piece de resistance was dessert, a huge cake in the shape of the Maybach car, complete with windows, wheels, fenders and all the other auto attributes. Elizabeth's nephew deserved a Michelin star for the meal. He did have a little help from his aunt.

Two minutes after the last drop of coffee had been swallowed, our guests got up, bowed, shook hands and whatever else was customary in their exotic countries. My Dutch friend gave me a huge bear hug, a kiss and an invitation to visit him at the lodge he had just bought in South Africa. I guess Ferris wheels are a lucrative business.

Since driving back to Cannes in their chauffeured Maybachs would have taken too long, at least an hour, and cut into their shopping time, they were to leave by helicopter. Five helicopters stood ready in the field about 200 meters from our house. But getting there required marching in the dirt, single file, through the vineyards. Reminded me of photos I had seen of the evacuation in Viet Nam, the difference being the Manolos and the Louis Vuiton and Prada bags.

We were allowed to keep all the leftovers which fed us for the three days. Two weeks later we received a check and a very flowery thank you from the German director in Stuttgart. Never heard again from my Dutch Ferris wheel magnate.

The longest and certainly the most profitable gigs of our house was the making of a four-part television series - *Le mirroir de l'eau* (mirror of water). Sent out in episodes of 100 minutes in August, such programs are traditional summer French fare. The cliff hanging "what happens next?" element guarantees a steady viewership in a dull summer TV season. Makes the advertisers very happy. It is absolutely necessary to have some big names, movie and TV, to achieve this. And one of the major stars was Our House!

One bright April morning at 8 AM the telephone rang. J who never opens an eye before 9 or 10, muttered a few unprintable expletives and picked up the phone with a very annoyed *"Oui."* Several more friendly *"Oui, Ouis"* followed. "Today at 4, no problem. Of course. Of course. *A cette après-midi."* (see you this afternoon)

"So what was that all about I?" I asked.

"You're not going to believe this," J answered now very wide awake and pulsing with energy. "They want to use our house as the main location for a summer series. Get up! We have to get the house in order." Like normally it's a pig sty.

"The house is fine. I'm going back to sleep." Precisely at four o'clock, our three dogs barking in unison announced the arrival of our new clients. We had been expecting one or maybe two people but a crew of five showed up – the producer, the director, the person in charge of the décor, a cameraman and for some reason I couldn't quite fathom, the makeup artist.

All men and, except for the makeup guy who was clothed totally in black leather, and the cameraman in sweatpants and a hoodie, the others could have been players in their own film. In designer jeans, blue blazer, white shirt opened to the third button to display masculine cleavage and chest hair, they were the epitome of French male chic.

After a few pleasantries and strong expressos, J took them around, extolling, the wonderful qualities of our house, its surroundings, the garden, the pool, the *colombier,* (dovecote) the gallery and even some rooms above the wine cave which I have never entered since I have a horror of all the disgusting things probably living there.

They came back into the house whispering among themselves. J, totally unfazed, invited them into the living room, offered the usual rosé and asked them to make their proposal as if it already was a fait accompli. Actually it was.

The director, the handsomest of this French movie delegation, started the conversation by announcing, "We would like to start filming next week."

I almost choked on my wine. "Really," said J, "that's rather short notice. May I ask? Did you have another location that fell through at the last minute?"

There was dead silence. After a bit of throat clearing, the producer admitted that this was the case. "Ah, but we are so glad. This house is much more suitable. And, so nice for you to be able to be part of the project."

Another "really" from J. I could see the commercial wheels turning in his head. "They are desperate. Good. Puts us in a great bargaining position."

I was starting to have serious doubts and broke J's golden rule about not asking too many questions until the financial details had been settled. "Exactly what does this project involve, how long, how many people and what is the film about?" I had suddenly morphed from server of refreshments into an annoyance. But J was proud of me and nodded. Showed we were not overly anxious.

The producer, a rather charming man, told us they would need the entire house, except for our bedroom and office for six weeks. Four weeks of filming, one week before to install all the equipment, change the entire décor of the house and one week after to put it all back in order.

There would be no extras hauled off the streets of Marseille for group scenes, only the actors hired for the series. Very famous actors and actresses. More about this later. They would arrange an office in the *colombier* (our converted pigeon house), use the gallery for dressing and makeup purposes and would set up tents and a food wagon below in our now dormant vegetable garden to feed the crew. We would also be invited to participate since our own kitchen would be off limits.

My first reaction was to say, "Thank you very much for asking but no thanks." J however was mentally rubbing his hands together. "Sounds wonderful," said J. You are really so lucky to have found such a perfect location. Shall we discuss the financial side." Another long silence.

"You are right," said the director, "we are lucky to have found such a wonderful house and therefore we would like to make a generous offer." He named a sum. J looked at him with a big smile. The producer grinned back happily.

"Triple it," said J, and you have a deal."

The producer and director looked at each other, the decorator was already making notes on how he would change the living room and the makeup man ran his hand through his (sun) bleached hair. I guess they really were desperate. It took less than a minute for the producer to agree. *"C'est bien."* J looked crestfallen. I was sure he was thinking "I should have quadrupled it." To me it sounded like an enormous amount of money.

That being settled, J magnanimously opened a bottle of Moet et Chandon in place of the usual cheap bubbly we drink and proceeded to discuss the nitty gritty. I wanted to know the story line. Just to be sure it wasn't anything too weird involving aliens or gun toting gangsters.

"Nothing like that," the director assured me. "Although it does involve murder. The plot revolves around a murder of a young girl twenty years before. Her mother has never been able to accept what happened. She has kept the room exactly as it was. Oh, incidentally, we need a room we can more or less destroy – wallpaper peeling off the walls, spider webs, thick dust as if it hadn't been aired in all that time. We will completely restore it when we have finished filming." J and I looked at each other. One upstairs bedroom under a terrace had been inundated with water. Talk about peeling wallpaper, the whole ceiling was slowly descending onto the floor. We had been waiting for months for the insurance company to settle.

"I think we have the perfect room for you," said J.

I, however, felt my hair standing on end. Because in fact when we bought the house there was a room kept by *Madame* Boulet exactly as it was in the 60's when her daughter committed suicide. The coincidence gave me a creepy feeling. However, the sum we were getting helped dispel it.

With a glass in one hand and a pad of post-its in the other our blonde decorator began sticking his notes on various pieces of furniture, art, lamps, even the drapes in the living room. Then disappeared into the hall, the dining room.

"Our movers will be here day after tomorrow to take out your furniture and art. No, no don't worry. They are extremely careful." Obviously, our furniture and contemporary art were not the suitable decor for an aristocratic lady living in a typical elegant French (read stuffy and old fashioned) house.

As planned in the morning two days later, the movers came, emptied our living room, including drapes, the hall and a few bedrooms. The dining room and kitchen were acceptable as they were. In the afternoon the house was turned into a cliché of 19th century French chic, complete with brocade drapes, copies of Cézanne paintings and lots of gewgaws and overstuffed furniture. A statue of a blackamoor with outstretched hand holding a tray to receive visitors" cards did give our hall a certain chic. I briefly considered asking to buy it. J was horrified at the thought.

In the week that followed, our abode became a Hollywood film lot. Trucks, cables, lights, wires everywhere on the terrace. Even those cute folding director's chairs that you see in films about making movies were placed around. Dressing tables with light bulbs around the mirrors, racks of all sorts of masculine and feminine clothes, trunks filled with myriad jars of makeup, cartons of toilet paper and a stack of white fluffy towels were installed in the gallery, along with an enormous old leather chesterfield chair belonging to the make-up artist. I found out that it accompanies him on all his jobs to relieve stress. He was definitely a diva.

Our pigeon house took on a new life as an office with desks, a battery of computers, phones, a photocopy machine and three gorgeous young secretaries, one male. Our once vegetable garden now housed a huge tent filled with long tables and chairs. A converted truck served as the gourmet cuisine.

The cast was not the ordinary run of the mill TV actors but top stars of theatre and movies. Line Renaud, the most famous, was a veritable old trooper – literally. She recounted how she had conquered Las Vegas in the 60s, singing and dancing. A great friend of Jacques Chirac, still president during the film, she could sometimes be overheard exchanging pleasantries with him on her portable. At least that's what I gathered from the *"Oui Jacques. Non Jacques."*

In this rather convoluted story, she plays the role of the mother of the murdered girl. The deaf-mute guardian of the property, much younger than she, is her current lover. Talk about the odd couple. Some of the scenes were filmed in the rooms above our cave, where as an employee he lived, now transformed into a very modest apartment but at least rid of bats, mice and other former undesirable inhabitants.

Extremely professional, Line never once complained, not even when sent out to follow a cat in the cold at midnight wearing nothing but a flimsy nightgown. Pinxo fell totally in love with her, following her everywhere often to the consternation of the cameraman who very politely asked me to get rid of that "expletive" dog. He sat under her feet, receiving all kinds of tasty morsels during every meal.

The other actress also well-known, although admittedly not to us, was Christiana Reali, star of stage and films, cast as the sister of the murdered girl. Pinxo may have fallen for Line Renaud but J was totally enthralled by Christiana and I couldn't blame him. Brazilian by birth, she could have modeled tangas. She was beautiful at 7 o'clock in the morning without any makeup and nice to everyone. J engaged her in conversation at every opportunity and photographed her continually. She didn't seem to mind. I did but just a little bit.

Once the actual filming began, the crew would arrive any time from 5 to 7 in the morning. All three dogs had to sleep in our bedroom and began barking the moment they heard a step on the gravel. The only saving factor was a table set up with coffee, juice and fresh croissants. Gypsy disgraced herself one morning by pulling down the whole tray of croissants and leisurely devouring them. Being a huge, very imposing German Shepherd, no one dared to take the goodies away from her. I explained she was very gentle and would never bite. I don't think they believed me and just took the precaution in the future of putting edibles out of her reach. Gypsy was not into coffee or tea.

One doesn't need an exceptional memory to learn a part to act in the movies. The average spoken lines were about two sentences when the cry "Cut" rang out. If the director was satisfied, the actors continued with the next couple of sentences. If not, the same was repeated ad infinitum. J never tired of watching the process. After the first day, I hid out with a good book unless there was really some exciting action going on.

Six weeks of having your house invaded by what seemed like hundreds of people is wearying. There were a few respites. One was lunch and the other that, except for one weekend, everyone disappeared from Friday night until Monday morning, during which time we were allowed to use the kitchen providing we didn't disturb the décor.

Lunch was a true feast. Out of this converted caravan came the most delicious meals. And every day was different. The table d'hors d'oeuvres befitted a Michelin star restaurant. Tiny pizzas with goat cheese, shrimps in an avocado sauce, a myriad of salads from lentil to beet, fried mozzarella balls, anchovies, slices of ham and sausage were starters.

After came the main course from steak with French fries to marinated lamb or battered fried fish, depending on the chef's whim. Desert was always a fresh fruit salad for the weight watchers and chocolate mousse , apple pie and other forbidden sweets for the pigs like J and me. Red, rosé and white wines were on each table. The French have no compunction about drinking on the job.

Word soon got around about our house's fame. The secretary of our village's mayor called to ask if *Monsieur* le Maire could visit the set. He was immediately invited by J, along with his colleagues, for lunch. J even photographed him with Line Renaud and later asked her to autograph the photo, which he sent to the mayor. On a later visit, J saw the photo nicely framed in a place of honor on his desk. I doubt very much if the Parisian types working on the film were very impressed by a visit of the mayor of an obscure village in Provence.

Finally, it was over. The cables, cameras, computers, desks, wardrobe and other miscellaneous equipment were packed up, loaded on trucks and disappeared from our property. In true French fashion, everyone came and kissed us goodbye even the people we had barely spoken to. I thought J lingered a bit too long saying goodbye to Christiana. He has her telephone number and still talks about visiting her in Paris. The chef told us if we ever needed catering, he would be delighted to come back "It is so beautiful here," he said.

The next week the house was put back into the exact condition in which it was found. The decorator had taken pictures of everything. Even my CDs were organized in the right order. They arranged to have a painter come and repair the destroyed bedroom with any wallpaper we might choose. A big fat check was handed over to J by the director with a hug.

A few months later, our village hosted the *avant premiere* of the entire film, all 4 hours of it, in our local *salle de fête,* (a hall for all sorts of events), in which a large screen had been set up. The whole population attended since there had also been scenes shot in the primary school and various other locations in town.

At the end of the film, the mayor took the stage thanking the people of his village, reminding them how famous it would now be. Then to my intense embarrassment, he asked *Monsieur* and *Madame* Farber to stand up and profusely thanked us for offering up our house. I wanted to sink through the floor. J waved like Louis XIV.

EPILOGUE

THRIVING IN PROVENCE

It was a beautiful day in early October, perfectly blue sky and golden sunshine. A recent rain had washed the summer dust off all the plants. The cooler weather made the roses pick up their heads and produce new blooms, the grass was green again and the leaves were just starting to fall from the *platanes.* They make crackling sounds when you walk through them on the terrace. I can enjoy this sensation since I don't have to rake them. Poor Robert. I think he hates autumn. You cannot imagine the quantity of leaves thirteen plane trees lose. Sometimes nature helps with the task by sending a strong wind to blow them all into one heap. Otherwise he attacks them with a *souffler,* (leaf blowing device).

I take one of the last swims of the season in water approximately the temperature of my freezer. But, ah, the sensation when you come out, tingling from the cold, and dry off in the still hot sun. I lie down on my chaise lounge, reading a book just downloaded on my new Kindle, earplugs connected to Mozart on my iPhone, feeling very high tech. Pure paradise – until the dogs decide they want an early dinner.

I walk back to the house, wrapped in a terry cloth robe, to find Jules on the terrace, his summer rosé replaced by an autumnal red Cote de Provence. "Hi," he acknowledges my presence, barely looking up from his manuscript.   J was writing a new book, which makes him incommunicado for hours on end.

"Do you miss Amsterdam," I ask, hoping to get his attention. It did.

"Are you nuts?" He takes a long sip of his wine and goes back to editing.

I feed the dogs and slip a bit of *foie gras,* in their bowls. Life is so good.

Made in the USA
San Bernardino, CA
05 May 2020